GERTRUD ORFF
The Orff Music Therapy

Gertrud Orff

The Orff Music Therapy

Active furthering
of the development of the child

Twelve pages of pictures

Schott & Co. Ltd, London
48 Great Marlborough St, London W1V 2BN

B. Schott's Söhne, Mainz
Schott Music Corporation, New York

© 1974 Kindler Verlag GmbH, München
English Translation © 1980 Schott & Co. Ltd, London
English Translation by Margaret Murray
Edition No. 11427
ISBN 0901938 59 9

Printed in Great Britain by
Caligraving Limited, Thetford, Norfolk

Contents

Translator's note

For the sake of clarity the therapist in the text is always referred to as 'she' and the child as 'he'. This does not apply, of course, when we know that the child concerned is a girl.

Where Gertrud Orff's work has been with German-speaking children, I have sometimes quoted the German words spoken by the children in instances where I felt that the sound and letter structure of the words was of relevant interest. In these cases I have supplied a translation alongside. Similarly, in some of the song texts both languages are given. Elsewhere I have given an English equivalent to the original text.

There is frequent reference to 'tension' within the context of various group activities. This should be thought of as something positive, containing elements of excitement, involvement, anticipation and elevation. It is often a total group experience as well as an individual one.

I should like to thank Dr. Eva Frommer of the Department of Child and Family Psychiatry at St. Thomas' Hospital, London, for the help she has given me with medical terminology; however, she is not to be held responsible for any mistakes in this field that I may unwittingly have committed!

Preface
by Carl Orff

With her factual knowledge Gertrud Orff combines a natural gift for teaching.

An active colleague in the realisation of my *Music for Children*, she knows all the possibilities of this educational approach from the early stages onwards. She is therefore an eminently suitable person to write this book, which gives for the first time a glimpse of her extremely personal way of applying music therapy in the field of special education. Her own knowledge has been consolidated and complemented through long years of work with doctors, psychologists and teachers in special education both at home and abroad.

The following text should open up a new area of operation for the complete complex of Orff-Schulwerk, that, contained in it completely, is now made accessible by a creative spirit.

Diessen am Ammersee
14th March 1974   *Dr. Carl Orff*

The practical examples of Orff Music Therapy are a product of the work done in the years 1963–73 in the following Institutes and Schools:

Heckscher Nervenklinik für Kinder und Jugendliche, München (clinic for nervous disorders in children and young people)
EMR (educationally and mentally retarded) classes in Bellflower High School, Bellflower, California.
Elementary classes in one school each in Bellflower and Compton, California.
Cité des Enfants, St. Légier, Switzerland.
Heimsonderschule Offenstetten, Niederbayern
(Special residential school, Offenstetten, Lower Bavaria)
Kinderzentrum und Forschungsstelle für Soziale Pädiatrie und Jugendmedizin der Universität München.
(children's clinic and research station for social paediatrics and child medicine at Munich University).

These institutions are cordially thanked for giving me the opportunity of collecting, testing and developing experiences of practical work for the help of handicapped children. My thanks are particularly extended to Prof. Dr. Th. Hellbrügge, Director of the Kinderzentrum in Munich. Working together with doctors, psychologists and the numerous patients, it was possible to develop the Orff Music Therapy – the title was suggested by Prof. Hellbrügge – to its present state. The photographs illustrate some of the work at the Kinderzentrum in Munich with inpatients and outpatients.

Munich, May 1974   *Gertrud Orff*

1. Premise

Orff Music Therapy is a multi-sensory therapy. The use of musical material – phonetic-rhythmic speech, free and metric rhythm, movement, melos in speech and singing, the handling of instruments – is organised in such a way that it addresses itself to all the senses. Through these multi-sensory impulses it is also possible to make the attack just where an important sense organ is weak or damaged. In spontaneous creative activity the child should express himself freely, give form to his expression and use it in social relationships.

Orff Music Therapy can fortify other forms of therapy when it is intelligently coordinated with them. It can be used with mental and physical handicaps, with sense handicaps, with disturbances of behaviour, development of the ability to communicate, and with the autistic. The results of treatment are mostly excellent and with some individual children outstanding.

Orff Music Therapy has developed out of practical work. In the following pages some insight into the process is given, not yet completed, but with quite a way behind it. Experiments undertaken in the course of more than ten years intensive work with normal and handicapped children have led to results from which certain principles can be deduced. This book does not undertake to solve all problems and answer all questions. It is placed at the disposal of those who work with children in the medical-therapeutic field, and those for whom music appears helpful in furthering the development of disturbed or retarded children.

It was the Greeks who gave the words music therapy their special meaning. Our therapy is concerned with the two words *musiké* and therapy. *Musiké* meant a total presentation in word, sound and movement. (Our present word music has come to be associated only with the complex of organised sound.) Therapy included the nursing, care and healing of the patient.

I see a particular value of our music therapy in the practice of social experience that it offers. In an acoustical atmosphere of play, affirmation of self, understanding for others and social integration can be experienced, tested and confirmed.

Music therapy is an old therapy if not the oldest. From the Greeks we know that they distinguished between active and passive music therapy, used in a homeopathic and an allopathic way. Homeopathic: working with the handicap, using materials that produce reactions similar to those of the handicap; allopathic: working against the handicap, using materials that produce different reactions from those of the handicap. These four basic terms are used today and a distinction is made between them.

Plato's poetic description of music and movement in his *Laws* (790 d) reaches us as if carried on a bridge from child to child over thousands of years. For him movement is an elemental thing for very small children, particularly experienced movement. He makes it clear "that the body can stand all shocks and movements that are expected of it provided these do not lead to exhaustion." He therefore prescribes movement and not stillness to help children who cannot get to sleep – in fact homeopathy: "When mothers wish to bring their children who cannot sleep to a state of sleep, they do not make use of stillness, but just the opposite; they use movement, rocking the child in their arms, and are not silent, but hum some song or other and make music for the child."

Receptive music therapy has now replaced the term *passive music therapy*. The word receptive is used with justification: music is received, the patient is influenced by music. Music does actually affect something in us, our nervous system reacts, without our having to notice it, to this acoustically formed sequence. Thanks to a polygraph one can read the influence of music on a person attached to it in an experimental way. In galvanic skin response variations occur, the heart beats more quickly; in EEG (Electro-encephalogram) tests the alpha waves with higher amplitude disappear as the music begins and are replaced by the beta waves. Only the quantitative influence and not the qualitative is measured. The latter will resolve itself in discussion between therapist and patient. The treatment with receptive therapy is particularly effective with adults, especially in cases of neurophysiological illnesses.

In the use of practical, *active music therapy* we find many different approaches today. Some believe that communal singing, others that instrumental ensemble playing is more productive. With some we recognise an overestimation of the value of sound in relation to a form of many sounds, with others an overemphasis on rhythm.

10

Within the framework three complexes of treatment reveal themselves: therapy in Pediatrics (children); therapy for adults; therapy in Geriatrics (the elderly). It is still the case that more adults are treated than children.

2. The Orff Music Therapy
and its relationship to Orff-Schulwerk*

The therapy that we call Orff MusicTherapy is new. It is closely related to Orff-Schulwerk and has developed from it.

The word Schulwerk indicates that it has to do with schools, that it has an educational function. One can begin with it in pre-school. Schulwerk also implies that we are looking into Carl Orff's workshop. Carl Orff's essential, artistic declaration of intent is given and can be found in his Schulwerk.

Carl Orff also says of his Schulwerk, that has the subtitle Music for Children: "the call, the rhyme, the word, the song were decisive factors. Movement, singing and playing become a unity: elemental music, elemental instrumentarium, elemental word and movement forms. Elemental music is never music alone but forms a unity with movement, dance and speech. It is music that one makes oneself, in which one takes part not as a listener but as a participant. It is unsophisticated, uses no big forms, is near the earth, natural, physical, within the range of everyone to learn it and to experience it, and suitable for the child." The five Orff-Schulwerk volumes are conceived as material for interpretation, and as models for one's own composition and improvisation.

Orff MusicTherapy adopts the idea of spontaneous, creative music making and makes use of the Instrumentarium that was designed for use in Orff-Schulwerk. These instruments provide a material of which full use can be made. Active music therapy is now a possibility with children. The type and form of the so-called Orff instruments makes a treatment for children possible.

Not all the instruments that belong to Orff-Schulwerk were "invented" by Carl Orff. There have always been drums, triangles and jingles. The melodic percussion, of which the xylophones present the greatest attraction, have their origins in Africa and East Asia, but Carl Orff has presented them to us in a new form in his Schulwerk – as Maria Montessori presented her material. She did not "invent" the right-angle and the triangle, but she made them educationally and therapeutically effective. She did not invent

* Orff-Schulwerk, *Musik für Kinder*. Verlag B. Schott's Söhne, Mainz.

scales for weighing substances but used these therapeutically. Children are already familiar at home with the element of water, and with using it for washing (are they really?), but Maria Montessori made a therapy out of washing with water. Similarly Carl Orff with his instruments, many of which he had specially built for us, has made an educational idea effective.

This Orff-Schulwerk idea has been varied and applied to the field of therapy. We have gained a threefold use of the material, the instrumentarium:

1. There is the possibility of acoustic-active participation.
2. The material acts as a *link* between therapist and child, as distancer and as a binding force.
3. With the material the child can communicate, can have social practice. Here too the material has a double function of bringing together and keeping at a distance.

In applying the material a threefold non-verbal communication is possible:

1. From the child to the material
2. From the child to the therapist via the material
3. From one child to another child.

If we look closely we can see that the Orff Music Therapy has always been housed in the kernel of Orff-Schulwerk itself. All creative activity with Orff-Schulwerk has its therapeutic aspects, but how and where can we bring to light the creative value that lies at its heart? It requires a humane teacher who is also factually trained. The therapy requires a therapist who is a naturally gifted teacher of children who in addition must have medical and musical training. There are countless institutions in Europe and in the U.S.A., which, equipped with an ensemble of Orff instruments, have attempted the therapy with children.

Starting point

The Orff Music Therapy has developed organically out of Orff-Schulwerk.

The Orff-Schulwerk idea was to create for children a complete dimension of music within which the child can express himself, experience himself as a person, and make music with others.

The therapy developed from this idea of a 'dimension of music'. It includes the same means. The child's levels of expression are language, rhythm, melos, movement, experience of space, all coordinated with one another. The material for this was newly developed. The child's creative expression as recommended in Orff-Schulwerk becomes the creative stimulus per se in the therapy. The finished models that one finds in the Orff-Schulwerk volumes cannot be used in therapy with a handicapped child. In only a very few cases could one recommend the exact imitation of a rhythm or a melodic line, let alone the execution of a complicated ostinato exercise. A mentally handicapped child can perhaps perceive a harmonic structure, but can seldom carry it out without help.

This does not mean that we shall never get beyond an absolutely simple basis, that we must always be restricting ourselves. We have to find a completely new starting point.

Our starting point is the child. The handicapped child is there in front of us and we have to find access to him. Being handicapped also always implies isolation, isolation through being different from others. Handicap, however, is also a relatively hopeful word. Take the handicap away and you have the child. It is the task of the therapist to penetrate through to the child. Unobtrusively.

The therapist must approach the child with alertness, and observe with sensitivity where a point of access presents itself. This is valid for the individual child as well as for a group of children. One cannot demand communication, it must happen. One cannot bring about eye contact by compulsion. Eye contact arises naturally, as a gift. When there is enough attentiveness there, when the child feels he can trust the therapist and the situation sufficiently, then eye contact arises of itself. I believe that when a child refuses to give eye contact, when he has not the strength to look the other in the eye, then the therapist should rather be shy too, and only look at the child indirectly. The first full glance should come from the child.

Material

The material that the therapist offers helps to establish communication. The material should so stimulate that it leads to a willing acceptance. I say 'material' deliberately. It rests with the imagination and intuition of the therapist (and one needs some luck as well) to start with the right material, or quickly to change it if the first attempt does not produce results. It can be an entirely non-acoustic object, if there is such a thing. I mean something offering tactile experience: a piece of paper, a bird's feather; or offering an experience of scent: a flower, an ointment. The first encounter should produce such a preliminary contact, of which the child gives visible evidence of his approval through small signs such as exclamations, smiles, glances, movements. The therapist must strive for this with inventiveness even in obstinate cases.

Because of the differences between one person and another, and between one handicap and another, it is not possible to give literal instructions, or to give a positive programme, suitable for every case. From case to case one has to decide anew, warily and quickly. Some fundamental general directions, certain norms and relatively well-known principles will be described later in the section that deals with the different handicaps. The therapist should develop a charismatic basic attitude of her own; it will benefit her gift of observation and inventiveness.

The therapy situation

Although one must make every effort in the first session to establish communication, in subsequent sessions there should be as little pressure of time as possible. Here everything should develop at an individual speed in relation to the child's capacity. Each session should be an experience in itself on which one can build. A session should form a unity. When the seed of the interest has been sown and the therapist has been accepted, everything will develop a step at a time.

The treatment sets itself no aim, at least not a preconceived one. The conscientious therapist will set an individual goal for each child, and when that has been reached, a further one. The treatment occurs as a process, metaphorically as a walk along a path. The winding paths are to be given preference, those kinds of paths along which children like walking. The direction, the 'whither', is certainly indicated by the therapist. She will accompany the child on all detours and byways, and will linger where a lingering place presents itself.

The winding path is not a direct one but it is full of life. It has unprotected places and therefore needs safeguarding. The winding path is flexible like the winding river that bends round the mountain. The most radical of straight paths is the tunnel. Seeming secure, and at least short, it excludes everything that stands in its way. It is therefore without life. He who walks or drives through a tunnel is confronted unexpectedly with a new situation to which he has contributed nothing. The natural, winding path is exacting but strengthening.

One introduces an idea or a material imagining that it will be accepted. Where the idea stimulates outward signs that come from the child, then this idea should be followed. If disturbing elements arise, intentionally or unintentionally, these should not be ligatured or corrected, but should be built upon or perhaps recast. This demands a tireless technique of the therapist. In appearing to yield she nevertheless keeps the control in her hands. But she must also allow herself to be surprised and genuinely to follow where such a surprise may lead. These are very decisive moments in the therapy that demand virtuosity (= virtue!) from the therapist. Instantaneous reactions are necessary.

These unforeseen moments occur because the therapy is a stimulus, a help for the handicapped child, and not a successive arrangement of programmes. Both therapist and child feel refreshed after being in contact in a situation that is built upon a swaying equilibrium. All participants feel, mostly unconsciously, how important their contribution is to maintaining the balance and the play situation.

The attributes of play include the ordered, the predeterimined, and the unordered and undetermined. In this tension the play takes its course. The ordered part consists of: the playing area, the limited space and in many cases the limited time available.

With us the allotted time is the session that occurs once a week

16

in a familiar and prepared room, to which children – provided they are having outpatient treatment – and the therapist come from various directions. Maintaining the tension from week to week is possible. In my long experience all the children have been able to retain the memory of the session as an event in their lives for the whole week. In the present climate of change and long weekends, etc., this means much. The distractions are numerous and the chances 1:84, if one counts up the hours of the day and their possible influences. The tension of some sessions can last for months. A girl aged five once had a gap of four months between treatments. She had a high IQ but could not concentrate, her behaviour was disturbed and she was also an epileptic. She was introduced into the music therapy as a preparation for the demands that school was going to make on her. She was in a group for four sessions during which she noticeably progressed from one session to the next, from totally unco-operative behaviour to a concentrated achievement. She came again and stood expectantly in the doorway. The time span of four months had slipped away. She held her ground with remarkable co-operation and had lost none of the positive adjustment that she had formerly achieved.

What makes the session so significant? Among other things I think it is the tension factor that is inherent in the play. It must be maintained, it is sensitive. "The essence of play is unstable. At any moment 'normal life' can demand its rights, whether it be a prod from without . . . or from within through a loss of the play 'reality' through disappointment or disenchantment."★

In a session that runs well we achieve a self-developing state of elevation which is inherent in a good play atmosphere. This state is in itself a factor for healing. It eludes an apparent explanation, is not transparent, but can be experienced. The children and the therapist sense at once when this state is not reached. This can happen, and, if it remains as an isolated case it is nothing to worry about. On the contrary, the inner effort to achieve once more a 'high' session is then the unspoken and often unconscious desire of everyone. In my experience the tension curve is also not constant but rather oscillates in waves.

★ J. Huizinga, *Homo ludens* 1939. Pantheon, Amsterdam.

Means

What is it that makes possible the unusual, the elevation, the tension, the arch that connects one time to the next?

Our music therapy is a dimension. It should be effective through the potential of its elemental character. Its elements are sound and movement, working together in a stimulating play situation. It has a beginning, a getting on board, a taking part, an ending, a within and a without. It is a continuous alternation between tension and release. The repeating, often and often, of the theme that keeps recurring, the wide range of different sounds, the tone colours, the strong impulses, the gentle stroking, the dryer moments, and the chain of movement, all of us, now only you, now me again, short rhythmic phrases, only accents, long phrases that become almost a condition, this whole richness of into one another and with one another, this happening that each one mirrors in himself and that he can see in the others, all this produces *fascination*. In the broader sense it is therapy through fascination. The technique, that with which we bring this about, our activity if you will, is fulfilled in this moment, for it is done with intensity. Refinements and improvements come about with repetition. Clumsiness becomes less clumsy, expression through speech improves. It is important, for instance, that a child with a speech handicap now wants to speak and does so. Every correction given at that moment would produce a sudden fall from this elevation and would be very dangerous. We each contribute everything that we can. Sometimes it is very, very little: think of a quadrispastic (see picture L top) who is perhaps also blind and mentally handicapped, but can nevertheless achieve elevation. It is all relative.

We start from the senses, those that we possess, that we are left with. The therapy engages all the senses, and where one sense is absent, compensates with another. The co-ordination of the senses is prepared for in our brain. We can read in Otto Detlev Creutzfeld's *Hirnforschung und Psychiatrie* (Brain Research and Psychiatry) that the stimulation of a nerve cell is conducted onwards to other nerve cells over neuron, nerve fibre or axon in the form of a series of impulses that are in proportion to the stimulus. On the brain surface it arrives at a projection of the environment and is in fact separated for the visual, auditory and tactile aspects of the environ-

18

ment. Already on the way to the cortex, however, and there in heightened form, it comes to various nuclei leading to a cross connection between the individual tracts.

The means in our therapy permit and demand a multi-sensory approach. The impulses are compellingly offered in a stimulating and fascinating way. In modern brain research (Creutzfeld) it has been recognised that it is the function of the neuron to make decisions, and that, unlike a computor, it does not process every signal. Each signal has to pass over a 'threshold'. If the stimulus is too weak the signal is rendered inactive. Only when the impulse is strong enough to carry it over this threshold can it become active. This is, of course, particularly the case when inhibitions and handicaps are present.

Our means are not only in the form of instruments that stand like a colourful palette before us, and that we touch and play; they are in us and around us. In this sense the means are of us: our own bodies, hands, fingers, feet, elbows, knuckles, nose, eyes. With verbal support all this is to be experienced by touching, clapping, blowing – to name only some possibilities. It helps in the recognition of one's own body structure: what belongs to me and where is it?

Means to be found within us: the experience of vibration when we hum, speak or sing. Means to be found around us: the space that we explore acoustically and as resistance, and that around where we are sitting, the differences to be found there, the mat we are sitting on, the floor itself, how does the floor sound when we walk, when we run. How does the wall sound, the door, the window, the cupboard: can you hear the difference? Innumerable possibilities for tactile and acoustic exploration can be found that benefit aural and visual experience and the recognition of things. There is a children's game in which hiding next to me, over me, behind me is 'not allowed'. We can reverse this and say: over me, under me, next to me, behind me – is allowed!

The multi-sensory use of means therefore applies to things in the environment, to ourselves and to the instruments. The therapist has to decide in advance which material to use, why it should be used and in what way it should be explored. She will prepare it and lead the activity in this direction. In her preparation she will always be finding hurdles and barriers within herself to be jumped over or removed; when, for instance, she wants to say to a difficult group or

19

an individual case: "There's really nothing you can do there." It is just such situations as these that can be turned to good account through using her inventive ability to open up new possibilities for herself and therefore for the child. I don't believe there is any case where there is nothing more that can be done; a smile or the passing shadow of a smile rewards the effort. One may well ask how smiles can be given where the severest handicap makes nearly every form of expression impossible. It is especially the minutest reactions in cases of severe handicap that appear hopeless, that are the most rewarding to the therapist. It is simultaneously the sensitive points where minimal progress is possible for the child. The severe handicaps of body and mind, however, do not predominate in the music therapy situation unless one works with those under intensive care. In cases with less severe damage we can tackle the problems and help with more noticeable success, and here there are also more readily available means and ways that can be shown, since similar cases can be treated similarly.

The many kinds of therapeutic means at our disposal are according to their essence, agents, whose effective power will be individually more closely described.

3. The therapy's specific agent

Instrumentarium

The instrumental material, taken over from Orff-Schulwerk is a key item in the therapy. Therapeutically it can be viewed from three starting points: tactile, visual and acoustic. The combination of these three sense categories makes a three-fold therapeutic effect possible. It also means that where a sense is defective or non-existent it can be compensated or stimulated by another.

1. *Applying the instruments for tactile use in therapy*
We have four main kinds of raw material: wood, skin, metal and strings. Further additional material such as sand, small stones, cork, cane and glass etc. is available. The following tactile characteristics can be noticed: Temperature (metal – rather cold; wood – less cold; skin – warmer)

Surface texture (wood, metal – rather smooth; skin – less smooth)
Hardness (wood and metal somewhat harder than string or skin)
Weight (wood is lighter than a corresponding mass of metal)
Elasticity (the differences of tension on skin and string instruments)
Vibration (metal vibrates rather more strongly than wood. If one takes a metallophone note from one of the barred instruments and holds it, where the hole has been drilled, between thumb and index or middle finger, one can feel the vibrations with the remaining fingers as one strikes it with a beater. Vibrations can be felt in this way with longer wooden bars as well).

Playing the instrument by touch without a beater, using only the fingers, or the palm or back of the hand, gives a range of tactile experiences from the general to the finely discriminating. The change-over from touching, pressing and handling without producing sound, and touching and handling with sound production, also gives a different kind of sense experience.

2. *Applying the instruments for visual use in therapy*
The instruments are made in different sizes: large, medium and small;

and in different shapes: round, rectangular, triangular, in the shape of a stick and in combinations of these forms.

We have large and small round objects, particularly with the various sizes of drum, most of which are held hanging vertically in the hand, though they can also be held horizontally or be placed horizontally on table or floor. Timpani are round and are always set set up horizontally. Then there is the large, round cymbal, and smaller cymbals up to the smallest finger cymbals. Ball-shaped rattles such as maracas give us the round shape in three-dimensional form.

Rectangular shapes are provided by the different sized woodblocks and, (with a reduction in size at the upper end) by the large rectangular shape of the barred instruments (xylophones and metallophones) with their resonance boxes, each with its interior, hollow space, and the bars themselves that give a clear visual impression of the differences in pitch.

Stick-like shapes are provided by claves of various sizes (made of solid wood or bamboo) and also the handles of the various beaters with their rounded heads.

The triangle is so named because of its equilateral shape with its empty space within.

The visual application of this material is valid for its own sake, but also as a contrast to the acoustic. In such a contrast it is the naturally silent situation that it produces, which is nevertheless filled out with activity, that is most therapeutically effective. With a beater in each hand shapes can be executed in space that can give up to three-dimensional experiences. On the floor, limited perhaps to from two to five sticks or bars, a series of two-dimensional geometrical figures can be shown.

3. *Applying the instruments for acoustic use in therapy*

One can remove the bars from the instruments to experience the specific tone colour of the individual materials: wood on wood, metal on wood, a string maintained under tension and plucked. The specific tone colour of these individual materials, wood, metal, etc., acquires its own qualified sound through the particular structure of the instrument concerned: skin is stretched over a circular frame and becomes a drum or kettle drum (timpani);

strings are stretched over a resonance box to make a violin or guitar. Related lengths of wood, each tuned to a certain pitch, are laid across a resonance box to produce the specific tone colour of a xylophone. A metallophone is made in the same way. Stone can also be tuned to different pitches, but here it is not the length but the thickness that determines the pitch.

With these instruments we have a rich palette of tone colours. The instruments can be used homogenously, using instruments from only one group, or heterogenously, using instruments from different kinds of groups. They can be used as a group or individually. We can put dark, low-pitched sounds together and contrast these with bright, high-pitched sounds. We can make dynamic differences between soft and loud, etc.

The instruments can be played and experienced in a pre-melodic way, without any recognisable melodic shape, and even in a pre-rhythmic way, without a particular rhythm. This is an important therapeutic starting point that can be carried out non-verbally and without rules, with its individual rhythmic structure and intensity. This kind of starting-point encourages activity and a willingness to join in in those who are inclined to be inactive, and helps the active child particularly, for he does not have to wait or to relate to a partner, but can take part and, with growing experience, can develop patience and concentration. This kind of polyphony provides a positive experience for individuals and for the group. Some kind of binding theme makes it possible. Felix Hoerburger* distinguishes various factors within the elemental pre-forms of polyphony to be found in folk music throughout the world.

In what other ways can we make use of the instrumentarium? Are there obligatory rules? Are there correspondingly identical uses for the various handicaps? Are distinctions made between individual and group therapy, between different ages? Should one introduce the instruments in a particular order? Are there recommendations for developing the technique of playing them? There are answers to all these questions, but not the answer. Some

* Hoerburger, F.: *Elementare Vorformen der Mehrstimmigkeit.* Orff-Institut, Jahrbuch III, B. Schott's Söhne, Mainz.

fundamental rules can be given:

1. An instrument conveys meaning
2. An instrument should not be used in a perverted way
3. The instruments should be used economically
4. An instrument can take over the function of a signal
5. There should be exchange and interchange in the handling of the material.

General application of the instrumentarium

1. *An instrument conveys meaning*

An instrument should be used significantly and according to its specific qualities. From what has already been said we see that each instrument has a multi-dimensional function: tactile, visual and acoustic. The tactile-acoustic function will help the blind, the tactile-visual the deaf, and the mentally handicapped will be helped through the acoustic to the other two. Above all, however, each instrument can be associated with a particular idea. We as therapists can and should let the instruments, according to their shape and their acoustical properties, be associated with and represent things or characters, but should not impose these upon a child. A child's imagination is often unexpectedly different, and it changes too. In this particular session it may be so oriented that it associates the sound of a triangle with a fish and not with a bird. One should naturally yield to this, for the child's auditory and visual symbolic associations will only come from his own world and experience.

The large cymbal, held hanging and struck with a soft beater, represents the sun for one group, and a tree for another. For many groups it is a 'sound-roof', and then it is struck, and, while still ringing, is held over the heads of a small group.

The association of an instrument with a thing or an event extends the sense capacity. It has a communicative character.

2. *An instrument should not be used in a perverted way*

One often hears that drums should be introduced with care because they can be played too loudly. A drum must sometimes by played loudly, if possible when there is a special reason for doing so. An example of perverted use would be the case of a melodic barred instrument from which all but individual bars had been removed.* This is perhaps acceptable in music education, so that the required notes can be more easily found and more accurately played. In the therapy situation this is impracticable. Small children and the mentally handicapped need something that is whole. A child that has only some rudimentary parts of a barred instrument in front of him will group them together, that is to say he will take them out and place them side by side, a fine motor task over which he mostly has insufficient control.

Playing freely on all the notes is entirely justifiable from an acoustic and tone quality point of view when the association or motivation is right. It then has a favourable effect if B flat is substituted for B natural. One thus eliminates the leading note in the middle of the instrument. Playing freely on all notes of the instrument is justified through the binding element of a common idea, a common phrase-length or something similar. It is diametrically opposed to an unco-ordinated, uncontrolled venting of pent-up energy on the instrument, which has little therapeutic value. It is the function of the therapist to co-ordinate the ideas, to bind together the imagination and the desire to express. It will then be possible to play loudly on each instrument since there will be a reason for doing so. This reason will also provide grounds for reducing the sound level once more. This will then not be disappointing, but necessary. The soft playing can then become loud and powerful again.

The effectiveness of the therapy bears a close relationship to the genuineness of the therapeutic approach.

3. *The instruments should be used economically*
It is of fundamental importance that the material for a session be prepared. This is particularly important for beginning stages and for small children. A selection has to be made and too many things should not be presented at once. A therapist who offers a small child

---

* If one wants to work with only a few notes one should use individual chime bars (resonator bells). Two or three chime bars are then a whole in this context.

a bass drum, two large timpani, various tambours, a pair of bongo drums and various small hand percussion instruments all at once is overwhelming him with material. She cannot excuse herself by saying that this is what the child wanted because he saw all these instruments in the cupboard. If one starts by allowing the child too much free choice he will, through his drive towards activity, try to do too many things. His attention span for one object remains minimal, no creative attitude is developed, the material is squandered. A situation very quickly develops in which beaters, and even instruments, are thrown around and the group can no longer be controlled or directed. One cannot shift the responsibility for the mismanaged situation by blaming the children. An exclusively tolerant or permissive attitude without any stimulation, has the same effect. The idea that one should intentionally leave the children without any rules to explore the instruments with one another is, I believe, quite wrong for this kind of therapy. It is time squandered and gives unsatisfactory motivation for further work. It is true that every creative process produces order from apparent disorder, but where there is chaos it is inevitably bound up with the process. An economic use of material is no restriction, it enriches. A paradox is created: limited material produces an abundance, too much material a surfeit.

Limiting the material produces concentration and stimulates the imagination.

4. *The instrument can take over the function of a signal*

The use of signals – the instrument tells you something that you must do – has a strongly binding effect within a group. It is divided into the designation, the execution and the acceptance of the signals. Their execution, where the tone quality of the instrument invites a particular reaction, should soon be given to a child. Where there is severely disturbed behaviour of a provocative nature the undertaking of active responsibility mostly produces miraculous results. The therapist will find that the use of the signal function will be most illuminating. The instruments can also be used as visual signals. This will be particularly effective where there is impaired perception. The non-verbal communication that is present in this kind of activity reinforces the atmosphere and the attention of group or individual.

Work with signals demands flexibility, the making of decisions and the taking of responsibility. These tasks have a communicative value.

5. *The material should be interchangeable*
During a therapy session there may be only one instrument in use and each individual uses it for only a short time. This is difficult to achieve with small children but it is possible. Social readiness to share can be awakened very early.

Sounds can also be exchanged, one can give them or pass them on. One can, for example, strike a small cymbal and put someone else into this orbit of sound by holding the cymbal close to their ear. It is a good idea if the therapist says at the same time: "Give him (or her) the sound!" The child who has given the sound can tell by their shining eyes that the other is hearing it. In this way he participates through the other, but without hearing. Another possibility would be that a child with a drum walks round a circle of children and gives each one in passing 'a cluster of raindrops' or something else, by gently tapping the drum with his fingers as he holds it over their heads.

The interchange of material demands and encourages social tolerance and spontaneous performance at the right time.

27

The perception of the instrumentarium

I hear and I forget,
I see and I remember,
I do and I understand.
Chinese proverb

The child is confronted with the instrumentarium, his senses are engaged, and he reacts, in three ways: seeing, hearing and doing. With our material we can complete a circle between these human senses.

1. *How does the child react to the instrumental material when it conveys meaning?*
Can a child accept that the large cymbal is the sun, that the sound of a triangle is a bird call, can he give a tangible picture of flowers on a glockenspiel? All this is possible as some examples will show.

Example 1

In a class of ten mentally handicapped children from a special residential school that I once visited – aged about 8 to 9 years and with an IQ said to be about 40 – it was possible to conjure up flowers by means of a glockenspiel. All the children fell in with the idea and they were even prepared to accept an instrument that was arranged in a pentatonic scale. It looked like this:

pentatonic	I I I I I I I I I I
with all the bars on, for comparison	I I I I I I I I I I I I

This arrangement is more distinct than the one with all the bars on. One can more easily gain a visual impression of a melodic pattern, one can recognise it again. In front of the children I took out the fourth and seventh degrees of the scale and also the fourth of the upper scale (F, B and F). I asked the children if this was all right and they accepted it. Now, going round the circle each child was asked to name a flower and to make a sound for their flower on the instrument. We had a violet, a sunflower and a tulip. Then came a child who pointed to a foliage plant that stood by the window. I nearly didn't accept this. Had I not accepted it as a flower the whole flow and tension would probably have been disrupted. The names were spoken clumsily with rough voices, or indistinctly and quietly. Not so on the instrument! Each child played his flower on the glockenspiel in a recognisable pattern. No child limited himself to a syllable pattern, two sounds for tu-lip, for example. There were melodic tendrils and in our imagination there stood before us a large and blooming sunflower. No child had ever played the instrument before so he was handling it for the first time. The tension held until all the children had expressed themselves, no child broke out and tried to play anything else. Each child was asked to repeat his first attempt immediately so that he could make a mental note of the phrase. When it was possible we also sang it. The therapist supported the atmosphere by saying: "What a beautiful flower yours is," "What a big flower yours is" and so on without implying value judgements. Now we had to try to play the same flowers again, and each child should remember his own. The group should also remember for we all wanted to participate. It succeeded. The association flower–glockenspiel was accepted and admirably executed. It raised the spirits of the whole group. On the following day they painted their flowers and sent them to me at home. The therapeutic teachers who were watching could not understand how a group with such a low IQ could have achieved such a concentrated performance. The regular teachers of the school classes were able in part to gain an entirely new insight into the behaviour and disposition of these children through their individual performances. A little girl, for example, usually the slowest child in the group, was very much on the spot in these activities and it was she who provided an accompaniment in the fastest time unit (quavers/eighth notes). Each child was allowed to choose whether the recorder should play slowly or fast for him, and he could choose how he would accompany on a drum. This girl not only asked for a fast piece on the recorder, but she also accompanied it in the same note values, something that no one else in this group did. At the end of the lesson it was possible to synchronise the individual time units in the accompaniment, so that the recorder was accompanied by minims, crotchets and quavers (half, quarter and eighth notes). If one had tried to impose such a rhythmic differentiation one would only have achieved it after weeks of practice. It worked so easily because the children were playing the unit of their choice.

Therapeutic features
Mentally handicapped children's common concentration on a theme
Individual achievement of a small form, use of imagination
Ability to repeat a form from memory
Communication within a group
Maintaining the tension
Deciding on a tempo and an independent accompaniment

Example 2

In a home in west Switzerland, during a course for therapeutic teachers I gave a demonstration therapy session with a group of severely mentally handicapped children with additional considerable behaviour disturbance. Each child had a turn at playing a triangle between the verses of a song.

Trois pi-geons sur ma tê-te, trois pi-geons sur ma main
Three pi-geons on my head, three pi-geons on my hand.

The verse was sung and the triangle played. I made no association between the triangle and the *pigeons*. The triangle functioned as interchangeable material and its possibilities were at the same time being explored. On the following day, in a second demonstration session when we were again about to use the triangle but in a different context, Marcel said: "ah, l'oiseau!" (ah! the bird!).

Therapeutic features
Sensitisation through tone quality with those who have acute behaviour disturbance and considerably retarded development.

30

Spontaneous association, restriction to one instrument, but freedom of choice on, and circulation of, the instrument.

Example 3

In a lesson with children (mentally retarded and stutterers) a poem with diminishing images was chosen so that different instruments could be used one after the other. The children chose the following representations:

There was once a large garden	large cymbal
and in the garden there was a tree	drum
and in the tree there was a nest	triangle
and in the nest an egg	finger cymbals
and in the egg a bird	sleigh bells
. . . and it's hatched out!	tremolo on all instruments

The children had to restrict themselves and make their contribution only at the prescribed moment. A visiting student said to me that this was really not the right sort of material, without rhyme, in a free rhythm and with no action, etc. The next lesson took place a week later. Already as they were coming in M. said: "I'll be the tree again today", and another: "and I the bird", and so on. They fetched their instruments and performed the same version of the poem without asking questions and without hesitation. The idea of repeating it had been theirs.

Therapeutic features
Stutterers can speak a short sentence fluently, they are motivated by the production of their own sound; in tension they think the next one's sentence internally; tension aimed at the common finish.

2. *Can an instrument in the hand of a child be perverted at all?*

Example 4

I remember a group of second grade American children with

31

whom I made a dramatic version of a Mother Goose poem:

One, two, three,
Four and five,
I caught a hare alive;
Six, seven, eight,
Nine and ten,
I let him go again.

The hare was represented and ran round in a circle until the signal
to catch him was sounded. I had imagined a beat on a timpani, hand
drum or some similar instrument. I was just about to suggest this
to the children but held back and asked: "With which instrument
will you catch it?" The boy considered and then went to the
metallophone and played many gentle sounds and then stopped. I
understood: he caressed the hare as he caught it, this was no
brutal seizure. How quickly an adult can debase an imaginative
idea.

Therapeutic features
Role play
Communication through group activity
Deciding about the musical signal.

3. *Is the child aware that the instruments are being used economically and
does this use of them satisfy him?*

Example 5

An American class again, this time fifth grade. We didn't have many
instruments but 35 children. Individual groups that formed themselves each received a barred instrument. The first group had the
task of making a musical statement with only two notes of their
own choice, the next group similarly but with three notes, the
third with four notes and the last with five notes. The solution
with two notes was not very satisfying, the one with three notes
turned out very well, that with four notes was no better. As it
came to the turn of the group with five notes one of them said:
"Can't we use only three notes too?"

Therapeutic features
Creating a form within set limitations
At the same time these limitations are voluntarily accepted.

Example 6

I would also describe the conversation on two timpani between two six-year-old boys as economical. They belonged to a group of stutterers and they were to think of what they wanted to say internally and reproduce it externally on the drums.

It was a scene about buying shoes. One bought, the other sold. The roles were allotted in a second. To the question: "Who is the buyer?" one of them answered spontaneously: "I am", "Who will sell?" "I will". The therapist asked a direct question and got a direct answer. The boys didn't change their minds either, for only one of them actually had any choice. Then the dialogue started, cautiously at first, a few sounds here – a few sounds there – one sound here – several sounds there – then it became very dense, with longer phrases and answers full of meaning. Each one allowed the other sufficient time for his response and neither interrupted the other. The fact that one of them was also spastic made the precision of his drum beats all the more astonishing. Finally they arrived at a definite ending and, without communicating verbally, they were both quite sure as to whether the shoes had been sold or not. Those who were listening and watching were not so sure, but it was not the making clear of the right answer that was important but the involvement, reacting to one another in this imaginary acoustic scene. The merriment that was released when someone made a mistake – "and he didn't buy them" – served only to further the social communication.

Therapeutic features
Co-ordination within the group, divided into the actively involved and the audience.
Training the imagination in two ways,
through representing speech at a non-verbally communicative level on the timpani
Internal flow of speech as a help for spoken language
Concentration in communication.

4. *Does the signal function mean anything to the child and can he make use of it to express himself?*

Example 7

In a mixed group that included some hearing-handicapped children the timpani gave the signal for different ways of travelling: slow walk, fast walk, skipping, jumping, etc. A single beat on the drum indicated a jump into a crouching position, and, after a period of silence left to the discretion of the player, a further beat indicated a jump back to the upright position. During these exercises it was particularly noticeable that it was the two hearing-handicapped children who were particularly good, both at playing the drum as well as taking in the sounds and translating them into movement. Playing the signal oneself certainly helped in perceiving its tone quality. One powerful boy, when it was his turn, played the drum with very gentle strokes that were almost inaudible, and the children walked correspondingly quietly. As he stopped he said: "But they didn't do what the drum said!" "What did the drum mean then?" "Where it went very soft they should have walked on tiptoe." We did it once more. He had identified himself so much with the drum that he had said: "They didn't do what the drum said."

Therapeutic features
Nonverbal communication through signals, sensitisation through listening.
Sense reinforcement for the hearing-handicapped.

Example 8

This group of children (aged 4 – 5 years) had an acute 'agnosia' (they hear but do not understand, for them language has no meaning. Hearing loss is often associated with this handicap. The children in this group didn't speak at all). Only through their visual sense could they be brought into a game sequence that they could then understand. But even here their attentiveness was minimal. One had to proceed with extreme clarity: Two tambours were held by two therapists to make a 'door' – the therapists stood side by side each holding the drum with his hand stretched out to the side, one to the right, the other to the left. The drums could move and they represented a kind of folding door. Once an adult had shown them how to bang the rhythm – o-pen door! – on one of the drums, they repeated this again and again with delight. After each 'knocking' on the drum the door opened spontaneously and clearly, each therapist taking one side step and close to the right and left respectively, and drawing their drums away from the centre.

Large, clear movements, speaking the words with great intensity every time they were drummed, helped the children to synchronise words and actions. The concepts "open, shut, door, walk, again" were worked at and associated with hearing and doing. There were countless repetitions. The sequence had three components:

1. The resolve to do it (at first a great obstacle)
   Conception
2. The action itself, the knocking on the drum
   Execution
3. The realisation, the effect: the door opens and one can walk through
   Result

Therapeutic features
Strengthening the impulses through intensification of the sense impressions.

5. *Can the child tolerate the exchange of material and does he gain from this experience?*

Example 9

In the group that has already been mentioned where each child played a solo on a triangle between each sung verse (see example 2, page 30) a mongol girl played and played on the triangle and showed no inclination to pass it on. She was the fourth in the group and three children were still waiting for their turn to play their solo. The therapist considered whether she should interrupt and say:

"That's enough, the others also want to play". Instead she only said: "You're playing beautifully – fine" – on and on rang the triangle. Afterwards the time was checked from memory – even fifteen seconds seems a long time, but I believe it was a full minute before the child stopped. Not really a long time, but within the framework of our piece, too long. With one last ring, that gave no advance indication that it was to be the last – no ritardando, just simply coming to an end – she stopped and contentedly passed the triangle on. Next day this girl took part in all activities with the other children and no longer took more than her share of time. Perhaps the fact that she was allowed to have this one long turn helped her to limit herself and to exchange time with the others.

Therapeutic features
Mongol child experiences 'time' and responsibility for her time.

Example 10

In a group of ten children from a home, brought together in a kindergarten and aged about four years, one instrument only was being used. This instrument, the soprano metallophone, stood in the centre of the circle of children seated on the floor. One child, 'the player', sat at the metallophone, ready to play. Opposite him, on the other side of the metallophone, sat another child, 'the beater-holder'. 'The player' had to play after we had sung and played our song.

The children could not count and so numbers and clock time meant nothing to them (the last line of the original German rhyme says: when the bells ring eight o'clock; "wenn die Veitglocke schlägt" is a substitution) but the "Veitglocke" (St. Vitus' bell) could ring. The beater-holder or bell-holder was introduced so that 'the player' was not over-taxed by having to wait, probably fidgeting restlessly, until at last the song is finished and he may play the bells. The beater-holder should hold the beaters conspicuously upright and when the song was over he gave them to the player. There were some excellent beater-holders among these children. The fine distinction between "you are the beater-holder" and

Hei-li- ger Sankt Veit,   weck mich zur rech-ten Zeit.
Wake me in the morning, please   get me up on time.

hand gestures

clapping

spoken

nicht zu früh und nicht zu spät,   wenn die Veit-glok-ke schlägt.
not too soon and not too late,   when the church bells ring.

Improvisation

D.C.

"hold the beaters for him so that he does not play too soon" brought about the successful playing of this role. Once the bells had been played the children changed – the beater-holder became player, the player went back to the circle and there was a new beater-holder.

The soprano metallophone was introduced here for the first time and at the same time connected with the idea of bells. It was set up with the full diatonic range of notes (with B flat instead of B natural). Each child played his own bell individually, each brought his solo to an end, more or less consciously, but he did it for himself. This activity gives insight into the children's behaviour. Not one of them was like any other, nor did they imitate one another in the way the played, but they did pick up and develop ideas from one another.

37

The fact that everyone sang the verse held the group together. The alternatives of soon and late were confirmed with gestures:

"not too soon"
one hand is lifted to the side and the words are spoken in this direction
"not too late"
the other hand is lifted correspondingly and the words are spoken in that direction
"when the church bells ring"
the hands come together in clapping.

Here, too, thirty seconds can seem a long time for the individual bell playing. As therapist one must tolerate this, it is worth it. When a child may play on his own, and may also decide for himself when to stop, he has the satisfaction of playing and also of having been responsible for a certain amount of time.

Therapeutic features
Tolerance within the group
Own responsibility for playing in terms of rhythmic structure, tempo and quality.

Speech

> . . . j'adore un Dieu palpable
> *Teilhard de Chardin*

Speech is an essential part of Orff-Schulwerk and is introduced there as a rhythmic-sound quality element. In the therapy speech is handled from the same basis. Often, however, speech is not there, or the understanding of it is lacking. The therapist has to create a fascinating, acoustic-speech atmosphere, with meaningful, significant visual support. The child must feel full of expectancy for something that is going to happen, so that at least his attention is directed towards this happening.

Speech can be introduced as 1. *rhythmic sequence* or as 2. *meditative condition*. Speech that is full of strong consonants such as r, s, t is seldom interpreted freely in a meditative way – it will have a strong, rhythmic character.

Example

Rab, Rab, Dürrbein,	Raven, raven scraggyleg,
d'Leute sagn, du hast nur ein'	people say you've only one,
ein Bein, ein Bein	only one, only one.

This verse starts by emphasising the consonant R – and these Rs should be rolled as if there were two or three of them together – and goes on to emphasise S in the second line and O and N in the third line (EI and N in the German).This third line belongs to the second, meditative category. The rhyme starts loud and rhythmic and finishes as if contemplating "only one" (leg) (ein Bein in the German). The strong tension at the beginning gives way and shades off in a ritardando. This may seem to be a rather involved explanation for such a small rhyme, but in this way it has life.

All speech material should be palpable, formative and graphic. There is no need to start by telling a story about a raven, perhaps in an autumn field. The material should make an impression of itself even when it is perhaps not entirely understood. Phonetic sound is more important than semantics in this work. In her preparation of a text the therapist should explore its possibilities along these lines and penetrate to its core. The significant high points or planes, colours or moments of monotony must be brought to life in sound. These exaggerations are more likely to reach the latent and rather indifferent sense of hearing of those who are handicapped in speech or hearing, to stimulate and gain access. The dramatic potential in the child should be accosted.

Here is a second example, with a strong rhythmic emphasis but rather a quiet one. It can grow to a forte and diminish again in relation to the dynamic shape of more and more ducks, whose pleasure in walking barefoot is obviously related to the volume of sound. Here we see the power of sound volume, how an increase in volume produces intensity and can assume a reality. Here one sees

39

the therapeutic value of the introduction of acoustical phenomena:

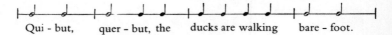

Qui - but,   quer - but, the   ducks are walking   bare - foot.

Another example from the German Orff-Schulwerk, Volume I p. 68:

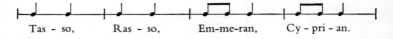

Tas - so,   Ras - so,   Em-me-ran,   Cy - pri - an.

Four names – with strong consonants. In my mind they suggest a procession of many people. They come from one side, march past and go out the other side. This produces the following situation: the expectation that they are coming, the appearance, the climax, they pass by us, they get further and further away, they disappear. Perhaps they will come again? Yes! There they are again. From these four names a scene is conjured up, the repetition of the names has some sense behind it, a gradual increase in volume takes place and the subsequent decrease in volume arises organically. The silence that is felt as the procession disappears, with everyone imagining that they can no longer see them – this has a strong binding effect on the group.

In contrast there is the meditative interpretation, spoken in a free rhythm, one can linger over over line, exaggerate every vowel. The suggestive power lies in colouring the vowels and in a slow performance:

Ein Haus voll,	House full,★	A house full,★★
ein Land voll,	yard full,	a hole full,
und am End ist's	you can't catch	and you cannot gather
keine Hand voll.	a spoonful.	a bowl full.

A child's drive towards play is also satisfied by playing with speech. Mentally handicapped children often have an elemental relation-

★   Traditional American version of this riddle.
★★   Traditional English version—answer: mist or smoke.

ship to language that sounds well or is rhythmic in structure. They can become attached to a word that has a beautiful or a strange sound. The inherent melodic quality of speech can be shown in just one word and thus brought to consciousness. We play with the word 'chinchilla':*

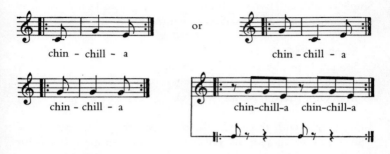

chin - chill - a   or   chin - chill - a

chin - chill - a   chin-chill-a   chin-chill-a

The speaking voice corresponds more or less to the intervals.

The inherent melody of speech is also noticeable in names. The most natural interval is certainly the minor third. Names can also be spoken in a rhythmic context with or without melody. One groups them then according to their phonetic quality.

Names beginning on the strong beat with three syllables (dactyl) in contrast to those beginning on a weak beat (anapaest).

Jennifer, Benedict, Hilary, Isabel

in contrast to

Matilda, Melissa, Fióna, Amanda – Tobías, Matthías
(piano)   (forte)

Here, in contrast to 'Tasso-Rasso' mentioned earlier, the names are only spoken according to their rhythmic syllabic pattern, being at present concerned with the structure and syllabic elements of speech.

* *Zikade* was the German word used by the author.

The up-beat iambic pattern is mostly to be found in girls' names of French origin:

Alíne, Iréne, Coléttte, Odétte

Single syllable and two syllable names starting with a stress (trochee) are prevalent in most lists of boys' names:

Stephen, Patrick, Thomas, Peter,
Joseph, Humphrey, Godfrey, Mark,
David, Andrew, Raymond, Roger,
Malcolm, Martin, Matthew, Paul.

Boy's names with three syllables occur less frequently nowadays. Those starting on a strong syllable are more common than those having a weak beat start:

Óliver, Chrístopher, Nícholas,

Orlándo, Sebástian, Nathánial

From proper names we should start to become aware of the melody of speech in "ordinary language". "Poetry contains all the elements of musical melody . . . poetry not only provides rhythms and suggests different pitches but with each of its syllables introduces new tone-colours."[*]

So we now have a natural relationship of speech to melodic intervals and to rhythm, the two essential components of music. This is exactly the enrichment that speech can give and in music therapy we can make use of these possibilities. Phonetic sound leaves the way open to semantic understanding. As we have already said we exaggerate to give clarity of form and to create an impression.

Rooooooose . . . . Phlox

[*] Gostaski, D.: the 3. Dimension of poetic Expression, in: The Musical Quarterly, New York, July 1969.

If one sustains a single syllable word like 'rose' for a long time it consists almost entirely of the vowel o, whereas in the word 'phlox' the consonants, particularly the final x, make one pronounce the o as a short sound. On the one hand a dark o, on the other an open one. A word like fish can be pronounced so that a long shshsh is immediately associated with water, duck . . short and faintly comic, stork . . as a large complete word in itself, finch . . something dainty and small. One can increase the dynamics of a word if one remains within the species and comes from fish to goldfish and swordfish, from finch to bullfinch, from nut to walnut and hazelnut.

Rhyme, where associated thoughts and associated sounds come together, is a phenomenon of language. The whole *Divina Commedia* is built on it. It is said that Dante invented the terzains whose three line stanzas stride onwards in a stirring rhyme scheme of aba bcb cdc ded etc., so that the new rhyme impulse is always embedded in the previous stanza. A translation cannot do this justice. "One can never know too many languages . . . with all respect to good translations – but no one can replace the original expression, and the original language in its word and phrase is already itself an historical statement of the highest degree."[*] In this kind of work a sense and liking for languages can be laid. The mentally handicapped child will mostly not recognise rhyme nor its apparent compulsion, nor will they perceive rhyme as a guiding thread to imagination and thought. As an example:

> You and me, me and you
> who's got money to buy an apple![**]
> some candy!

The non-completion of a rhyme does not disturb the mentally handicapped child at all. He does not get beyond his first thought, what he would now best like to buy, at the expense of the rhyme. He remains literal, realistic. He does not understand what 'lies behind', he does not think quickly ahead, he does not understand the joke. The understanding of rhyme, the ability to execute it can be appraised as a criterium for mental maturity.

[*] Burckhardt, J.: *Weltgeschichtliche Betrachtungen*.
[**] Original rhyme has 'a shoe' here.

Like an understanding of games, understanding of rhyme can be assessed as a positive factor within the framework of a test. Gotaski believes:

"Rhyme succeeds in introducing into poetry
1) the richness of musical tone-colours,
2) the logic of cadence,
3) the sublety of modulation and
4) the symbolic value of harmonies."

Spastics, who in general have little motivation towards movement, can be stimulated in this direction by speech impulses. The impulse of words, spoken in a suggestive tone of voice, supports hand control and movement generally.

All invitations to play that occur in a session should be consciously formed in language. They come then into the category of non-verbal invitations and belong to the game. One naturally avoids any artificial exaggerations.

Cross connections from rhythm to speech and from speech to rhythm should often be presented. The verbalisation of rhythm helps to understand and remember it. Transcribing verbal patterns onto a non-verbal rhythmic plane through clapping, walking, etc., produces tension, internalises the speech, a process that has a strong, communicative value when it is performed by a group. For the stutterer this is a way of performing speech internally at a fast speed and correctly, but at the same time externalising it through clapping its rhythm. Finally it helps the flow of speech.

Movement

The word movement in English, as in German, refers both to internal and external movement. The corresponding Latin word *motio*, movement, is related to *emotio*, inner movement or emotion. Both words come from the verb *movere*, to move.

With the handicapped child in general his capacity for movement is also impaired, the desire for movement is mostly dammed up – if we except the restless movements of the hypersensitive, easily distracted child – proportional movement is lacking. The inner movement towards something, the movement towards someone expressed in speech, in general the motivation to movement is lacking. In the most severe case, autism, it seems like a movement entirely directed inwards. Everything going outwards or coming from outside is parried. The stereotype movement of an autistic person, using the back of the hand and thus tapping with the back of the finger, is a warding off movement, a movement that pushes away from self; whereas the usual tapping movement has the palm of the hand towards the object concerned and is a movement of making contact in which exploring and touching are included. In English, as in German, there is an analogy between touching and being touched (in the emotional sense). An autistic person is untouched.

If movement is missing then the social factor is also missing. No contact with people or things is entered into. Turning towards someone or something in movement is not only motoric but also implies a change in the direction of attention.* Aggression is a perversion of social communication. Expressing oneself and focusing the associated movements in the direction of someone or something is a fundamental human characteristic, that, when it cannot express itself positively in the form of a dialogue, will express itself aggressively in anticipation of being repelled. Aggressive movement is often a perverted form of creative movement that has not been accepted. When we say "I will tackle it" in terms of "I will come to grips with it" – this is a positive metaphor.

The close connection between music and movement in our work helps movement and helps music. They are related to one another like lock and key. Because of the various handicaps the motor capacity is nearly always affected, and there are often only limited movement possibilities. But it is the musical means at our disposal that give motivation and release to these. In our work movement has various forms from mime and gesture, mostly non-locomotor, not moving from one spot, through locomotor movements that take you away from one spot in individual and rhythmically governed ways, up to the composition of movement sequences.

* Hassler, R.: *Hirnforschung und Psychiatrie,* publ. Colloquium.

When I point to myself and then to someone else within a rhythmic structure, and when I point upwards and then downwards, I have contrasted movements that I can use in the form of a musical canon, but I can also use them again for social purposes. If I walk (or run) supported by drum and recorder, I have a good rhythmic-motor exercise. But if a contrasting part is added in which I stand and clap to a partner, then the exercise is enormously enriched. I have to walk in such a way that when the recorder melody comes to an end I am standing by a partner (or not standing by a partner, according to the circumstances). This gives the walking a motivation. The clapping section with a partner can be the same length as the phrase for recorder and drum. This is possible with children who are not too severely handicapped. Making the phrase length the same lengthens the span of attention in that it relieves active attention because the equal phrase length is usually felt naturally.

Movement exercises in echo form – I clap, you clap after me – have a social value. There is an analogy between movement and expectation. If I, together with others, walk towards the centre of the circle, motivated by the rhythm and sound of the syllables

hu   hu   hu - le hu   hu   hu   hu - le hu

then, standing close with the others in the centre, walk backwards to the outside of the circle with the syllables

si   si   si - si si   si   si   si - si si

I have added a social experience to movement. If I add to this external sounds that are decoded by everyone together I strengthen the feeling of communication through tension and interconnection one with another. Nothing has to be explained; the non-verbal communication is there. When all other children sit or stand in a circle and one child walks round among them performing some rhythmic speech activity, this is an experience of self as opposed to others. It is strengthened by the fact of being alone. If one child may choose another through the call related to some kind of game, then the initiative to make decisions is strengthened. One becomes a good social companion when one can do things on one's own and make decisions – a prerequisite for social integration.

A movement that is not seen, or one that is only internally felt, giving hardly any outward visible sign that it has occurred, has a strong, socially communicative effect. By holding hands in a circle, for instance, one can create an electric circuit, one increases the current through pressure, one decreases it, one makes current impulses: a rhythmic unit is passed as a hand pressure travelling one way round the circle until it returns to the original sender. Is it still the same unit? Where did it change and why? Through incapacity, as a joke or through wanting to spoil the game? The therapist will react accordingly. If a circle of hands is not acceptable, perhaps a circle of feet can be tried. Everyone sits, their feet touching one another. As a contrast each drums on the floor with his feet. This alternation produces a soft-loud tension. One should not be afraid of the loud phase, the return to the electric circuit provides the guiding thread, for without it there would be electric shocks, such as would be beyond the control of the group. This electric circuit is not directed from outside but is controlled by the group themselves, and therein lies its therapeutic value. The contrast gives a balance. The loud outbursts, in this case the powerful drumming with the feet, act as a valve, but one that is under control. These dramatic effects are therapeutically effective, also effective with a group of healthy children. Here one can maintain a quiet tension using only the eyes, by blinking them, perhaps as a contrast to heavy stamping.

Movement sequences, initiated by one and copied immediately by the others as if they were mirrored reflections, gives the individual the responsibility for the movement and an experience of success. These are very conducive to communication.

Supplementary Material

Of the wealth of materials that can be used in this context I would like to describe just two possibilities in more detail: the use of small carpet squares as a way of organising the space, and various uses for hoops.

47

When we sit, we sit on the floor and most of our instruments are played from this position. We have a larger, smooth, single-coloured carpet measuring about two by two metres. We can use it as a place in the centre, a place for the little ones, or an intimate place for the older children. In addition we have a number of carpet squares in contrasting colours. One can place them to form a circle round the centre carpet, or they can form a rectangle, or two rows. The spatial arrangements are numerous and many associations can be made. They can represent islands or houses, one can make a carpet path of them or build a street between them. They can indicate 'outside' places for an individual, for several individuals or for everyone, and they can also be places for instruments or be used as natural movement boundaries. In all cases they represent a non-verbal invitation. They invite rhythmic walking patterns: walking in the spaces between; skipping on the carpets, stamping in the spaces; walking on tiptoe on the carpets, etc. When sitting on the carpets one can combine acoustic and visual effects by knocking on the floor in front of the carpet, on the carpet, behind and beside the carpet.

As the children come into the room they choose to place themselves on a red or white carpet and they call out: "I'm on red", "I'm on white". They call this out individually or together; the colours bind them together. The therapist now plays the recorder and the children walk about as long as they hear it. For this purpose it is a good idea to have the same ending to each phrase, to which one draws special attention and that might also be verbally underlined, and have a perfect cadence, perhaps as follows:

find a per-fect stop-ping place!

One can attach this melodic phrase to the end of various melodic variations so that the children listen for and expect the ending. They then place themselves on the nearest piece of carpet and call out again: "I'm on red", "I'm on white". An extension of this activity would be: "red moves, white stays still". Nothing further has to be explained, it is governed by the nature of the game and the rhythm. Many variations of this red–white idea are possible. One group of mentally handicapped children had great fun out of greeting one another thus: "Good morning Mr. Red", "Good morning Mrs. White!"

In a group of three to four-year-olds with impaired hearing we used one of these small carpets and laid a hoop round it and made it our 'waking-up place'. The game was organised as follows: the group of children are seated, playing chime bars (resonator bells), and as long as they continue to play one child walks around the circle clapping. When he no longer sees and hears them playing he goes to the prepared place with the hoop round it and, kneeling down, he 'goes to sleep' there. He cannot see us any more. When he hears the prearranged instrument, a triangle or a drum, he 'wakes up' with large gestures. His capacity for hearing is keyed up to this sequence of events and therefore assisted. An extension and an ending to this game was provided by one child; he spontaneously picked up his hoop and skipped around us and we clapped as he did so. It had now become a balanced three-part form.

A hoop was used successfully as a therapy instrument with a boy who was very ill. He suffered from the 'Lesch–Nyhan–Syndrome', and felt the compulsion continually to scratch himself on his face, hands and body. The aim of the therapy was so to interest him that he could forget his compulsion to scratch. Because there were several adults present, therapists and doctors, it was possible to build an 'acoustic atmosphere' on xylophones and glockenspiels, an obvious melody with accompaniment. He listened and was fascinated. As an interlude each person played two sounds on his instrument and asked him: "Who played then?" "You" he said, in barely intelligible speech, for his ability to speak was very limited, and pointed to the player. Later he joined in, very clumsily, with two sounds on the drum.

Now the hoop was used. The therapist made it turn round in the horizontal position to the accompaniment of shaken jingles and supported by the rhythmically spoken words: "Hoop, hoop, round you go", repeated over and over again. Once more he looked on from his wheel chair absolutely fascinated. A loudly spoken "Stop!" (Halt in German) interrupted the turning of the hoop. Soon the boy was saying the "Halt" himself. Since he usually spoke very seldom and with great hesitation, the frequency of the halts and the short intervals between them was quite sensational. He wanted to help to turn the hoop and we dared to unbandage one of his hands. He laid his hand on the hoop and called out the halts. Later he managed it with both hands. He took hold of a beater and played the cymbal. His movements were uncontrolled and spastic. It delighted him to stop the vibrating cymbal by grasping it with his hand, 'snapping' it. He said the word "snap" (schnapp in German) first and then stopped the sound by grasping the cymbal with both hands. These were small but active contributions. A hoop spinning round on one spot, touching the floor, getting louder until it finally came to rest amused him very much. On average this would last for about half a minute. "More" he said when the hoop lay still. He was able to watch this with maintained interest up to eight times, and the spinning place was always changed. When the hoop was once more near to him what he had seen reinforced his own turning movements.

The therapy was applied multi-dimensionally, even if with limited means: motor-rhythmic activity through turning the hoop, shaking the jingles, striking the cymbal or drum with verbal support. When in control of the game he also had to make decisions and he experienced expectation and its realisation. During these sessions he never scratched himself although his hands were unbandaged. Later it was possible to give him a form-board game with large shapes to complete. Here too the interest-tension was maintained so that he didn't scratch. The joy released by these activities and fulfilling experiences, and the accompanying tension may have influenced the secretions and chemical reactions.

In a group of older children with disturbed behaviour the following game was played: "Think of some place in the room where you want to be and go there when you hear the signal (claves, for instance), but don't change your mind!" This game should be played in silence, its surprise effect provides a good communication. Or: "Walk about as long as your hear the sound of the cymbal but organise your path of travel so that you are on your spot before the cymbal sound stops." (Spot = carpet squares distributed about the room.)

For a girl, aged seven, subject to epileptic fits, with disturbed behaviour and very restless, irritable and hypersensitive, the carpet squares arranged in a wide circle acted as a boundary to her running about, she saw them as a non-verbal indication. In order to bring her away from her stereotype running in circles the therapist stood "in the way". At first the girl didn't stop, but after a while she struck the offered drum with her hand. Later she remained standing beside the therapist, beat her drum and, following the therapist, made movements accordingly. Her stereotype running was now punctuated with breaks. At the beginning there were only two minutes of quiet sitting within a thirty minute session. Within three weeks this had increased to twenty minutes of quiet sitting in comparison with ten minutes organised running.

Hoops can also be used as enclosures: a small red carpet square, on it a hoop and within the hoop a glockenspiel – this makes a well-prepared place that helps concentration.

With a group of blind children this was a resting place that one reached at the end of a 'sound path' made of individual chime bars (resonator bells). A blind child plays his way along this sound path and comes to the resting place where the hoop is. Here he sits down and tries the glockenspiel. Perhaps he will have a visit from another blind child: he hears him coming along the sound path, perhaps the first child remains sitting by the second child. An echo game may take place, or a dialogue. With very small children the sound path is arranged without any system. With older children it can be constructed in thirds, fourths, or in different ways. This idea can also be adapted for use with children who can see.

4. Practical work

Co-ordination of materials

The co-ordination of materials has a special justification because of the functional interconnection of the sensory system. "The hypothesis of the unity of the organism is no empty phrase. The pathological condition of any one organism's functional system will be influenced by other functional systems . . . a pathological condition does not have to have been brought about only by a disturbance of the function of one or other of the organism's systems, but can also result from a disturbance of the interconnection between the systems, even when these individual systems, observed in isolation, show no noticeable deviation from the norm. The problem of the interrelationship of functions is one of the most important in contemporary biology and medicine."★

Because we are dealing with handicapped children whose senses and nature do not react directly, spontaneously or normally, we try to approach their senses and nature with several impulses at once, in the expectation that one stimulus or a complex of stimuli will make its mark.

Our overtures may call forth a direct reaction from the child. It may also precipitate itself within the child with, for the time being, no visible result. In some cases and with some children many impulses are needed. These are stored by the child, as if at the source of a spring, and then come spontaneously bubbling out, often, for the therapist, at the most unexpected moment. This means that the therapist should keep up the intensity of her approach, admittedly with varying impulses, of which one will effect a breakthrough to the child. If one has a success of this kind at the first encounter, so that the child shows by some external sign that contact has been established, one must carefully consider what it was that made this possible so that one can continue to make an effective approach of this kind.

★ Feigenberg, J. M.: *Funktionelle Verbindungen der sensorischen Systeme,* Hippokrates Verlag, Stuttgart, 1972.

The materials can now be organised as being

1. next to one another and after one another,
2. with one another and on top of one another.

The first arrangement is linear and after one another in time, the second is vertical and simultaneous. In the first case a whole can arise from specially prepared sections, a co-ordination from next to one another to into one another. In the second case, after a short explanation several entities are combined simultaneously.

Various elements are available to both linear and vertical co-ordination. These combine as follows:

speech and movement (gesture)
rhythm and speech
rhythm and movement etc.

Within these entities elemental co-ordination arises.

1. Linear co-ordination
This should always be used when the children cannot cope with too much all at once, or when a combination of tasks does not reach them at all, but rather confuses or inflicts damage. Complex demands cannot be made of an autistic child, he shuts himself off, is offended. Linear co-ordination is given to the mentally retarded, to mongol children, where concentration is weak and where behaviour is disturbed through brain damage. These children, however, are stimulated when they are allowed to take part receptively, that is watch without having too many demands made of them, while mildly handicapped or normal children perform a more complex activity. In a therapy situation where the children are selected one can build on those elements that have shown themselves to be receptive. Autistic children receive many peripheral or 'oblique' impressions from their environment without acknowledging it to themselves or to others. Linear co-ordination should be used in all cases where stepwise progress, repetition, work aimed at the condition of the child can be influential. Experi-

ences looked at from different points of view are gathered together into a whole and built upon.

2. Vertical co-ordination

makes complex demands and is always used when one wants to make an effect through intensive impulses,

- where impairment of the senses exists, in the hope that *one* sense will be reached,
- where there is aggressive behaviour disturbance, in order to gain their interest,
- with severe spastics and the physically handicapped, to give them motivation towards external self-expression.

The use of vertical co-ordination with those whose senses are damaged appears paradoxical. In a practical sense they will not receive all the impressions fully. Those with hearing handicaps will miss the auditory and those with visual handicaps will miss the visual. For those with hearing handicaps the auditory impression is made obvious through movement and thus compensated; for those with visual handicaps the visual impression can be experienced through the relative power of sound. Spatial distance is comprehended through the sense of hearing. The movement of sound in space affects the sound and gives structure to space, it is scanned acoustically.

With children with disturbed behaviour, or with those who cannot concentrate, one can go from a whole complex of activity to one part of it and work at accuracy of rhythm for instance, or sort out the different instrumental parts. Should there be a falling off in the atmosphere one can gather the interest again through vertical co-ordination, having worked at the individual parts they are put together once more into a whole.

A combined vertical co-ordination can be taken in by severe spastics, i.e. when the child listens and watches and is enthralled by an acoustic happening, best executed, when possible, by several therapists playing simultaneously. The child will be able to pick up some details, and though his contribution may be very, very limited it will be built into the already existing volume of sound.

He then identifies himself with this sound volume, refreshes himself with it, and it becomes a motivation and stimulation for further individual activity.

Vertical co-ordination can grow out of linear co-ordination, one does not, however, interrupt the flow. The individual elements, clapping, singing, speaking, and playing of instruments is learnt by everyone and performed by everyone, one element after the other. During the performance the individuals are told which part they will take when it is put together. The individual parts carry the tension, each knowing the structure of the whole.

Elementary co-ordination

Example: 2–5 years old

> Material: Speech, movement, instrument used visually, possibly also acoustically.
> For use with those who have little motivation, or with the mentally handicapped, but never with autistic children.
> "Drum, hide me!"   one holds a drum in front of one's face
> "Drum, beside me!" one takes the drum away sideways so that the face can look out again.

This exercise for partner relationship is effective when executed between therapist and child. It nearly always appeals and even severely mentally handicapped children react to it. "Drum, hide me" is spoken strongly (in German, "Trommel versteck") giving a firm impulse, and the drum is held in the hiding position for an indeterminate length of time, giving a pause before the second impulse, "drum, beside me" ("Trommel weg"), spoken with less intensity. The second pause is also free in length. Where a child is rather apathetic one makes the pauses irregular, so that every time a new impulse effect occurs and stimulates. With a restless child with disturbed behaviour one would make the pauses regular to give a stabilising effect. The accentuated first impulse that increases in volume and whose speaking pitch rises audibly (more so in German), is reversed with the falling interval of the second impulse, spoken without intensity. The first interval rises about a fifth from the fundamental note, and on the second impulse falls via the third back to the fundamental note.

In the second part of this activity the therapist retains the speaking part, the child gets the drum. The strongly accentuated speech now gives way to something more intimate, such as: "Drum, hide Marion, Marion's gone! – there she is again!" It is the suggestive way of speaking in the first stage that is responsible for the effect and the breakthrough. In a third stage one could sing and would then have worked on three planes, emotional, cognitive and abstract.

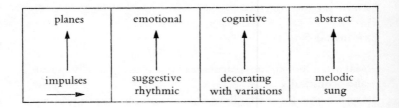

Linear co-ordination

Example: Age range 4–7 years old, all groups except those with visual handicaps

Material: speech, movement, drum
Therapeutic features: co-ordination, development of tolerance, individual contribution

"The drum goes round, don't you look round!"

a. The therapist is the first to walk round the circle of seated children. She is beating on a drum and at some point comes to rest standing by one of the children. This child now takes the drum and walks round, and so on.
b. All sit in a circle and speak the verse, clapping to it or tapping their knees or the floor.
c. An extension of gesture would be a rhythmic movement of the hands, first over the eyes, then away from the eyes

56

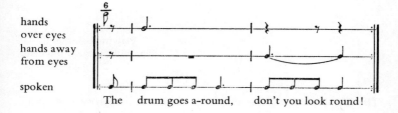

hands over eyes / hands away from eyes / spoken

The drum goes a-round, don't you look round!

A child now walks round the circle, while we speak the verse suggestively: "The drum goes around, don't you look round". He continues walking until he is standing by the child of his choice and then he says: "You look round!" The new child now takes the drum and does the same. If any child takes too long to make a choice it may help to make some kind of interjection such as: "Where will he stop?" In one group the seated children all had three or four claves or rhythm sticks, and while the child was walking round and the rhyme being spoken they would be making little structures with them. As two children changed places the one would carry on with the design the other had started.

For the therapist there is much to observe: handling the drum; the management of time; the choice itself, is it related to personal, game or social (choosing a child that has not yet had a turn) considerations?

Further examples of handling the materials and different ways of co-ordinating them will be found in the sections dealing with specific handicaps.

The individual materials are used in co-ordination, they are mutually enhancing and they intensify the statement. Just to combine two things is not necessarily an intensification, and the starting point should never be technical. One must consider a text carefully to be able really to intensify it with other means. One can use either the sense or the phonetic sound as a point of departure. One will discover a synthesis between sense and sound. One must discover the inherent, but not necessarily the obvious, rhythmic and melodic substance. There may be several possibilities.

Rules

Play implies interplay—
there must be give and take.
Marshall McLuhan

The therapist must work with her children with open eyes avoiding every routine. Even the way in which she talks to the children will differ from group to group. Groups that do not know one another should become a unity. They have been put together on account of their handicap, their age, and sometimes because of an enforced necessity. One should not be in too much of a hurry to get rid of those children who do not seem to fit in with the others. I also do not think it necessary to form a group round a nucleus of two children who already have some experience, in the expectation that they will help the others. I believe it is possible to integrate and develop equally a group of children that has been formed for the previously mentioned reasons. In any case, in practice one always has to take on new children and fit them into the group in the middle of a course of treatment.

The younger the children, the smaller the group should be. The number can almost increase by step with the age – three three-year-olds, four four-year-olds and so on. Only in exceptional circumstances should there be more than eight children in a therapy group. Three or four eight or ten-year-olds can naturally also make a good interactive group. There will never be an ideal situation in relation to size and make-up of a group.

All groups at every age should be thought of as groups that interact with one another in play. The therapist plays *with* the children in the game and is subject to its rules. Game and behaviour rules are not referred to directly, however, they should be disguised in the game. A plan must be prepared. The first session will be given to observation and assessment of the individuals. The children are observed in relation to their ability to operate and according to their behaviour one with another and towards the therapist. The results of this first session will tend to provide the plan for further sessions. The therapeutic aim has to be related to the situation of the group. The plan has to take into account the possibility of interaction.

We want to stimulate the group to make their own contributions and we want our plan to constitute an experience. We cannot exact this, it has to develop of itself.

The experiences to which all should come can be divided into three categories:

1. Experience of one's own personality
2. Experience of the structure of social life
3. Experience of physical reality

The three experiences interpenetrate one another so that the handling of an object can give an experience of one's own personality.

In relation to 1. In both the normal and handicapped child we want to prepare the ground for these three great dimensions of human experience. These experiences will grow in the course of life:

the awakening and strengthening of the ability to experience
the sense of discrimination,
the sense of association,
the development of sensitivity,
the sense of contrast and flow, i.e. rhythm in its broadest sense.

In relation to 2. On the social side we have to listen to and observe others in order to be able to understand them. We should develop

the capacity for tolerating others' actions,
the capacity to react through the senses,
the capacity to interact through the senses.

In relation to 3. In order to understand what kind of a physical world surrounds us in terms of tangible objects that have to be handled, developed, taken care of, we have to help the child to develop

an understanding for objects that are handed to him and of his responsibility for them,
an understanding for time and events in time,
an understanding for space and its penetration,

an understanding for order, form, consonance, dissonance and silence,

the experience of the interrelationship of the senses to one another.

If the therapist can provide an appropriate and pinpointed stimulation the development of these senses and capacities can be brought about. These means enable the child to be held firmly and yet to be resilient at the same time. He develops his own personality and a sense for social interaction and thus comes to terms with the world around him. Through the co-ordination of his own powers in the motor and emotional fields he is able to communicate, and from this an interaction develops.

It is the task of the therapist, by the way she uses her materials and through her own role as stimulator or controller, to further such a communication from which interaction can develop. She must switch herself on or off according to whether these conditions have to be prepared or maintained.

No corrections should interrupt the flow of what is happening. When a mild or a more severe correction is needed, however, the play situation can be restored by a well-chosen word that has some bearing on the activity concerned. The whole work is concerned with process and not with product. The fulfilment is found in the process or way. The method (Greek, methodos – the way) is to make the way interesting. A way always includes repose. The way should start at a suitable tempo. It also includes detours. The capacity to play, to become engaged in the game and the imagination that is necessary for this, these can count as test criteria. The child has the chance to take part on many levels. If because of a physical handicap he cannot fully take part – perhaps he cannot walk and jumping and walking are part of the game, then he can take a drum and give a rhythmic 'accompaniment' to the others as they walk or run. Or a child does not speak, or refuses to speak, but one sees in his eyes and in the way he otherwise behaves that he is fully in the spirit of the game. The moment will come when he joins in the speech as well. One does not condemn a negative contribution to a game, one values it as an example of contrast. Let us say that everyone is walking quickly, but one of them makes a point of walking slowly, or everyone is walking slowly and perhaps very quietly, and someone takes the advantage of making some quick, loud jumps. Our play must be flexible enough to tolerate such extensions. It is also toleration to choose the 'contraster' as a leader, or in some other game to make a special point of listening to what he has to say.

Relevant to this the interjection of a boy in the fifth grade in a school for black children in Compton, California, provided a very constructive moment, it was a perfect fit in rhythm and was thus built into the game. We spoke the following verse with gestures:

"I won't" came forth loudly from the far side. Perhaps he meant: "I won't cry in the evening because I laugh in the morning", or perhaps he didn't like the verse and its interpretation. These thoughts went quickly through my head as I saw how the black teachers who were present were addressing themselves angrily to the disturber of the peace. Already the "I won't" was coming from everyone on the side where the boy was standing. I immediately gave these boys my support in that I spoke it with them and, with every "I won't" I took one pace further into the centre of the circle. They went with me and their eyes lit up – they had won! From the centre of the circle we went backwards and as we did so the volume of sound decreased until, by the time we had got back to our original places all was quiet and silence fell; I had also won. It is the best situation in life when two people are content after a disagreement. It could have gone very badly and very usually – this was unusual and the forty children in the circle – a large circle! – seemed relaxed and all were ready for the next activity. The boy who had made the interjection was well-known as a disruptive element and was never accepted by his teachers. In this rhythmic activity he could gain a sense of achievement which was motivation for him. It is almost unbelievable, but it did make him better, he was more relaxed, and no more dependent only on creating a disturbance to gain attention.

To deal with disturbance factors one must go back to their causes: if they are creative in nature, one must try with the speed of lightning to see how they can acquire justification in terms of form. If they are defiant or merely negative in motivation one should ask if one has called forth this behaviour oneself, or what other reason may lie behind it. To what extent it may be external or more deeply rooted in the personality. It is just such visible alarms that give us the opportunity, because of such behaviour, to push forward and to consider ways and means by which these disturbances may be encountered effectively.

The therapist cannot always react correctly and make the right decision. If she looks back over the situation and relives it once more, she will be able to rethink the situation. If she takes this amount of trouble she will neutralise her previous ineptitude. Through such necessary reflection she will make herself more sensitive, and perhaps in another case, just because of this experience she will make a better decision.

The exploitation of the moment and the situation will provide the most secure stimulation and control. Through intense observation and quick decision-making one can find that the small contributions of the children, accidental or conscious, will provide a stimulus for the session, and the therapeutic material will then belong to those concerned in the session. If one incorporates the momentary situation one is more likely to set something in motion. The word and the idea moment has a connection with movement. In Latin momentum and movimentum (movement) are related and even have the same meaning. If we apprehend and comprehend the moment as impulse and possibility, something specific and unique takes place, something that engenders a movement, an emotional movement.

Technical form

The one thing we would all like is to have a *sure* technique. We want to take it over as acquired property that succeeds unfailingly when put into use. The original word 'technique' does not help us much in this context. In Greek it means 'art, skill' – the meaning ranges from art to the gift of prophecy, in general it means to occupy oneself in an intelligible way.

We nevertheless understand technique to mean a certain style of approaching something. It perfects itself in doing. Therapeutic work with a group requires a technique that is acquired and firm but at the same time flexible and spontaneous. The acquired experience must do justice to the moment. From the moment comes more experience. Therapist and child are both exposed to the technique.

Those captured moments within a span of time from which we learn – therapist and child – are significant for the new situation.

Consider the case of a child that always brought a doll with her and insisted that the doll must first play or react, so that only with the doll could anything be achieved. If that child comes one day and says: "I didn't bring Sascha today, I can actually play better without her", she came to this realisation through thinking about it at home during the week. She came to the session with her mind already made up and she gave voice to her decision. That is important. She did not put the doll on one side during a session because it had disturbed her.

The therapist makes use of technique and perfects it; the child is aware of technique to some extent and acquires it. We have three important categories for a session: the preparation, the way the session runs, the work done after the session.

The preparation is dependent upon the session that came before it, and this is pinned down in the work that follows. Consideration for a coming session moves in circles. A glimpse into the workshop of the mind will help us once more: the Greeks, particularly those

63

from Boeotia, called the first three muses: memoria, cantus, meditatio. What do these three words say to us?

memoria: memory, supports the power of thought, includes the cultivation of memory; it is knowledge of what has been done, worked at, experienced. It is concerned in time with the past. A condition of having.

cantus: song, has to do with singing, speaking and representation. Advantageous use of the remembered, the stored; it is a spontaneous, creative act, concerned in time with the present. A condition of being.

meditatio: in general, reflection, can include advance consideration, mental preparation for something yet to come, a condition of expectation, concerned in time with the future. A condition of becoming.

If we cultivate *memoria*, *cantus* and *meditatio* and allow them to become effective we have a correct and rounded technique.

When do we cultivate *memoria*?
In offering various materials in the fields of speech, movement and instrumental playing the memory is heightened, trained, consolidated through imitation. Since this should happen voluntarily there is affective support and its power to impress is considerable.

> Our activity must have so much reality and be so appealing that it has affective meaning. The activity must be carried along by the spontaneous desire to do it, otherwise the activity is meaningless, even though it may be correctly accomplished. Learning is affectively supported.

When do we have *cantus*?
Through the invitation to individual activity, creative or imitative, through the stimulation that can come through therapist or group, the activity is spurred on, given form in the present, the sense of reality is trained and through the interaction the self and the self's own abilities are recognised, confirmed, shaped. We are forming the capacity for assertion.

No correction interrupts the flow of events, wrong paths and detours are trodden together. Moments are observed in order to intervene to the best advantage. Learning is actively supported.

When is *meditatio* effective?
The work, the activity produces reflection. This is strengthened in the group through watching what the others are doing, through the resultant interaction, through the mirroring of one's own activity in that of the others. The point of view thus won helps for making decisions, for new solutions. Pauses in the activity, a condition of expectation, foster the powers of consideration. The meditative disposition is experienced.

Activity is both active and passive. If the assertive capacity is strengthened, new ideas can be won through reflection, deliberation over what has been done and presented. Learning is contemplatively supported.

The child learns then to come to terms with these three conditions: activity, forethought, reflection, and he learns their techniques. He learns to think both forwards and backwards from the moment. He learns about responsibility and consequences; he acquires a body of materials and experience.

One could illustrate this as follows:

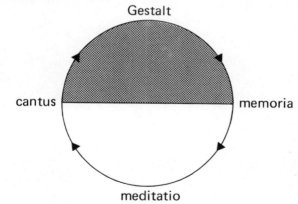

Every technique has developed from a process. It has distanced itself from the process and viewed it objectively. The acquired technique can be transmitted as a method. It is a concentrate from which everything to do with feeling has been removed so that it can be preserved. The method can be taken over if it is applied in a lively way and is similar to the original process. Therefore it is transmittable to a limited extent. The marrow of the method needs juice in order to flow, the method needs the contribution of an active human being. That which is suspended in liquid is flexible: if the therapist is flexible the plan will be flexible and the group will become flexible.

5. Therapy with different kinds of handicap

Practical examples

The following give some examples of forms of handicap or disturbed behaviour. Through being confronted in my work so far with many kinds of handicap, and with multiple handicaps, I have had to treat them all. The diversities of handicap have a common *and* a different starting point in the therapy plan, the same material and specific material. The extent of the handicap ranges from 'slight' to 'severe', the boundary between 'normal', 'healthy' and 'handicapped' is often blurred and cannot be clearly drawn.

The diagnosis made as a result of testing and case history should of course be broadly respected. It helps the therapist to sort the child into a specific group, or to decide that he should first have, or only have, individual therapy. The therapist should, however, be able to be flexible in relation to the diagnosis. There can be areas of reserve in the child, of a favourable or unfavourable nature, whose depths have so far not been plumbed by any diagnosis. Without relying on the diagnosis the therapist will allow the child to have an effect on her, and, out of the moment will offer him a challenge. She cannot be sure, and she should not expect to be, what the child's reaction will be. A child who has perhaps already been handed from one institution to the next, and who has often been diagnosed, will often present himself in such a way as to confirm the official verdict. A child can already show *the* mask that is expected of him and that hides another face. It should be a general policy that discussions about children between psychologists, doctors and therapists should only be entered into when the children are not present. Imprudently, however, such discussions are often conducted in the presence of the child, in the assumption that he will not understand any of it. It is no deception to realise how deeply hurtful, perhaps also 'satisfying' such words, that the child catches hold of and stores in undigested form, can be, and how they can influence his behaviour.

An experienced child psychiatrist* believes that even with severe mental handicap where a capacity for perception is lacking, a child can distinguish whether a discussion has a well-meaning attitude or one that is cold and factual, and that the child reacts to the latter with crying.

Since both adult and child are always exposed to change, a handicap will also be affected by this in some way. One should not capitulate before such a severe diagnosis as 'deaf' or 'blind' and mechanically treat the child as if he were deaf or blind. The therapist should be equally receptive to the moment of surprise as she offers it to the child.

Handicaps of the senses

Faced with a child with a sense handicap we can see that the handicap is not limited to the damaged sense but that it has also attacked corresponding motor and mental development. The human baby develops his senses in his mother's womb and is born with them working, but he comes "into the world, as the only case among vertebrates that is incapable of movement".**

In an undisturbed development, with the necessary stimuli from the environment, the child is formed and stamped, according to the cultural surroundings, within the first twelve months.** With receptive senses the human acquires his first experiences, through focusing, grasping, moving himself, touching, walking, etc. Through example he comes to imitation, spontaneous movement, and finally to speech.

If the child cannot take in the challenges and stimulus of the environment, either because they are not offered or because his senses are not fully receptive, then an external or an internal kind of sense damage arises. They can coincide. The mental development is dependent on the development of the senses and both have a corresponding effect in the field of motor activity. If this damage arises from external causes as in cases of deprivation (withdrawal

* Lutz, J.: *Probleme des behinderten Kindes,* Urban u. Schwarzenberg, München Berlin Wien, 1973.
** Portmann, A.: *Biologische Fragmente zu einer Lehre vom Menschen,* 1951.

of mother or mother-substitute, mostly through an institutional situation) then it can be repaired to a certain extent when tackled as soon as possible. With congenital, or pre-natally acquired sense damage, this damaged sense must be compensated through supplementary stimulus and challenge and an intensive therapeutic treatment must be entered into.

Defects of hearing and speech

An ear alone is not a being
John Cage

The person with a hearing handicap is nearly always socially handicapped as well. He lives isolated within a community, important information and signals from his environment pass him by. He does not quite belong to them, and some things don't belong to him. Sound is an essential part of existence and belongs to the flow and rhythm of life. Rhythmic activity can to some extent compensate for loss of sound experience because of their intimate relationship.

Hearing handicaps, that always bring with them a delay in speech development, are also accompanied by a general lack of relationship to the surroundings, to the subject and object world, and from this a lack of interest, a lack of desire to make contact with things and people arises. This paucity of contact encourages isolation. A child with defective hearing that has not yet been recognised is unjustly regarded as unresponsive, listless, inactive, even stupid. Lack of patience with the child because he does not 'listen' when we require something from him, will draw out an aggressive response. His movements are not normally co-ordinated, he bumps into things, he doesn't jump, or only clumsily, he is nervous of turning himself round because for him this rhythmic-motoric movement is not accompanied by any sound. From the beginning he lacks the natural resonance that would confirm his movement or even his activity. 'Half of life' is missing for him. Through rhythmic activity the child with damaged hearing is most likely to experience an access to sound. Unrecognised hearing impairment occurs more frequently than one thinks. That children with

69

damaged hearing compensate themselves visually is not always the case. They have to be specially trained for this to happen.

In music therapy the instrumental material, combined with a visible movement, acts as an agent for bringing understanding. Activities of this sort should be offered in plenty. The therapist must present an accoustically stimulating atmosphere, with meaningful, significant visual support. Being together in a group, that in addition is geared to a common activity, can offer a way out of isolation and encourage the way into society.

Every activity in the group: beating a drum, walking with a triangle, jumping to a drum beat, playing on instruments, brings the child with damaged hearing nearer to an acoustically alive life. To what extent these activities can be felt directly as acoustic is of secondary importance to the activity itself. Rhythmic units, executed with the hands in clapping, with the body in swaying, with the feet in walking and stamping, penetrate him and duplicate these vibrations within him. He does not only hear with his ears. The resonance of a drum surface, the vibrations of a floor caused through stamping and skipping, allow him to understand what had previously been closed to him.

Even the most minimal aural experience is important: when they experience it with *one* object, this awakens the interest in exploring other objects. "I can hear this thing, perhaps I can hear the other one too." The whole attitude to the object world can be changed. As we have already said it is not at all the case that the hearing handicapped child naturally compensates with his eyes. He has to be trained to do so. The therapist can often not understand how it can take so long for such a child to imitate an apparently simple movement. For this reason, when the child has achieved it, one remains longer with the same activity than usual, until it is so obviously natural that the child has some benefit in the repetition.

Example 1

A group of about four children, aged from three years, two therapists. A drum and then several drums.

The children stand in a loosely-formed circle, some distance from one another and in clearly defined places. While beating a drum the first therapist walks to the second therapist and tells her with clear gestures and verbally to take the drum to the next child. If the drum comes back to the therapist in this way she introduces a variation, holding the drum high as she takes it to the next, or holding the drum near to her ear as she strikes it, or banging the drum on her knee as she walks. It is fine when a child introduces a new variation. Eagerness in execution increases, certainly there will be some form of expression in vocal sound, they change places in the circle more quickly, the children understand the joke, they relax, they, laugh, they 'speak'.

After this experience of large, relaxing but intensive movements and crude sounds, one can come closer together for a more refined experience. The therapist holds the drum to her ear while she plays it, or after she has struck it. She listens to the vibrating drum, she encourages the children to do likewise in succession, and all watch the active child. For another child one can play the drum close to his ear, or for another play it over his head. Holding the drum for everyone to beat, and beating everyone else's drum gives a common experience of vibration. These suggestions are supported by a speech stimulus, that can turn into significantly rhythmic speech:

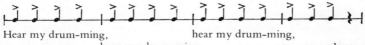

Hear my drum-ming,   hear my drum-ming,

       hear my drum-ming,   one, two, three

Everyone now has a drum

One can alternate: speaking and beating loudly with speaking and beating softly.
One can play alternately with the finger tips and on a particular part of one's own body. Again liveliness and jokes occur, two components that are extremely important.

A rhythmic verse

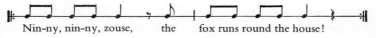

Nin-ny, nin-ny, zouse,   the   fox runs round the house!

can be played out. The seated children form a drum circle (each holds a drum in right and left hand) and they play their drums by banging the edge on the floor.

Drums

This gives a fine resonance and if the therapist speaks with intensity the children will try to speak with her. One child is the fox and he runs round the outside trying to get in. He must knock on one of the drums, the drum is lifted, and he is inside the circle, though there's not much space.

Again the action is supported with speech

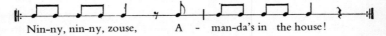

Nin-ny, nin-ny, zouse,   A - man-da's in the house!

Finally one lets all the children accompany the therapist's drumming with walking and skipping alternately, even if they cannot yet manage the latter. The two contrasted movements should be well supported both acoustically and visually.

Therapeutic features

Observation, imitation, tolerance. Through the increase of intensity that arises from the repetition and variations, one stimulates the emotional plane which makes vocal expression possible. Sitting close together in a circle intensifies both social and object contact; the speech should be supported with a precise rhythmic-motor activity.

Easing the tension but intensifying the rhythmic activity through moving in space, at the same time paying attention to signals. Need for social adaptation.

Example 2

Experience of sound and stillness, of differences of quality, awareness of form, vibration in the accompaniment.

72

Children aged three to five years – two therapists, individual chime bars (resonator bells).

Each child has two chime bars and together they all make up a chord of G major and create an acoustic atmosphere when played together. One can sing to this or play on a recorder. The end of the phrase should be clearly felt. Following this one of the children (in turn) walks, runs, jumps round the circle of playing children. At a signal, that comes irregularly, everyone stops together. This means that the dancing child is left high and dry without sound, and in this vacuum he quickly goes back to his place. When he gets there he is welcomed joyfully by everyone starting to play again.

After this contrast of sound and silence the chime bars are once more played in a circle and the therapist stimulates various rhythm patterns. She can indicate these, the same length as those played on the chime bars, by gesturing silently with beaters in the air, and then back once more to playing with full sound. One after the other the children can choose one of a collection of recorders that is held out to them, and that recorder will then play especially for them. The child plays his chime bar and matches his rhythm to that of the recorder. It is interesting to observe – contrary to popular belief – that many children with damaged hearing will particularly choose the smallest recorder, the sopranino, with the highest frequencies. This is noticeable in repeated cases. They also point to the recorder and want to hear it played if the therapist fails to do this during several sessions.

There follows an intensive experience of sound in that one holds the chime bar right up to the ear, feels the vibration and, if possible, distinguishes between high and low sounds relating these to the different lengths of the bars. One could call a child back from outside the circle by playing one of these sounds. Does he know who played it?

At the end of this session one can place the individual bars side by side according to length and put them on a table or other support so that they can be played while standing. Or one can use the large bass metallophone, if one has one. On account of its vibrations this latter instrument is particularly productive for those with hearing loss. Each child plays a few sounds. There are no rules except that each must allow 'space' in time for the others. An extension: the children spread out to the walls, and come in individually to the table or instrument when it seems right to them, they play a few notes and then go back to their original place. The result is a flowing coming and going and various sounds in free rhythm. (See B, top picture).

Therapeutic features
In going round the circle the child experiences the support of the sound and its absence – his reaction to this. Social behaviour of the rest of the group. Offering complex and differentiated hearing experiences. Social adaptation with an object alternately in space and time.

For further possibilities see examples 7 and 8, p. 34 and Supplementary material, p. 47.

Such groups can be homogenous or heterogenous. Children with speech handicaps but with intact hearing – backward in speech through deprivation (too little stimulation speechwise), stutterers, elective mutes, fit in quite well into a group of hearing-handicapped children, for every attempt at vocal expression within this reduced capacity for speech is valued and supported by the therapist. One does not include children who can speak, however, for they might then be regarded as something special or unusual.

The speech handicapped child must be continually stimulated to speak. Speech should become a necessity for him. All correction should be avoided at first, everything that he offers should be positively accepted. It helps to allow a stutterer to let a sentence flow indirectly, to let the timpani speak the verse rhythmically, for instance. Even spastic stutterers can produce a verse with rhythmic flow – they are speaking it internally at the same time (see example 6, p. 33). The relaxed atmosphere helps the stutterer, he feels free and without pressure and he achieves speech. Sung speech is in any case easier for the stutterer. If one reduces the singing to one recitative note, with emphasised words rising or falling in pitch one has come near to speech. Strongly rhythmic speech should also change quickly to everyday speech, for instance:

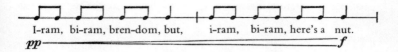

I-ram, bi-ram, bren-dom, but, i-ram, bi-ram, here's a nut.

pp ——————————————————————————— *f*

"What kind of a nut?"

Possible answers: "a monkey nut . . . a hazelnut . . . a walnut . . .". In gesture one can knock out a monkey nut, pick a hazelnut from the bush and see a walnut on the tree. It is just the change from taut, rhythmic speech to almost underplayed, light, everday speech that makes for its flexible handling. If one can capture the cadential pattern of a sentence (see p. 38, Speech) one can focus the tension to the end of the sentence:

I saw the apple – fall.
He throws a snowball at – me!
He throws a snowball at – you!
He throws the snowball – away!
Come now, or it'll be – too late!

Cadential melodies with dominant to tonic tension, not pentatonic ones, give tension followed by a final resolution. This is just what the stutterer lacks. Swaying, dance-like movements, and 'floating' also help a tense body.★

Speech is possible with 'Auditory Agnosia' if there is no additional impairment of hearing. But it cannot be called 'speech', it has no meaning and is mostly only echolalia, what is heard is echoed back in undigested form. Through acoustic movement games, through sharp contrasts, spontaneous speech can nevertheless be stimulated, provided that there is no accompanying mental handicap.

Tests with an audiometer, or EEG tests, can establish that the capacity to hear is present in children with a central disorganisation of perception, but it cannot be utilised. What is heard is not interpreted in the mind, is not understood. The connection to the central

★ Orff, G.: *Arbeit mit Stotterern*, Marhold Verlag, Berlin.

75

perception system is interrupted, what is heard cannot be made use of.

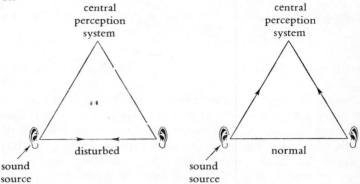

The purpose of the work is to give acoustic signals and to support them visually so that they can be identified with an example, even if they are only indifferently perceived either aurally or mentally. The reinforcement of a sense impression, the attaching of importance to small units is necessary (see also example 8, p. 34).

Speech is constantly stimulated with painstakingly detailed work, in the assumption that, with visual reinforcement, these speech building bricks will finally be recognised as speech.

In a group of four to five-year-old children who were at first completely mute, and who suffered from a central disorganisation of perception and were inactive and listless, there developed finally a syllabic form of speech – connected phonemes – connected sound units, unintelligible to us, but for the children surely a basis for communication, otherwise they would nor have reacted with 'answers'. This happened in the sixteenth of weekly music therapy sessions. This scene is by chance recorded on video tape:

The children stand by a large board and draw rhythmic symbols

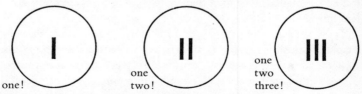

The circles represent the drums that were beaten

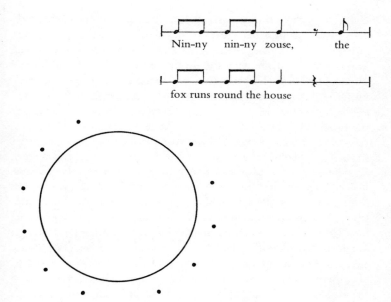

Nin-ny nin-ny zouse, the

fox runs round the house

The circle represents our seated circle, the 'tracks' are those of the fox or the child that walks round. The number of dots correspond to the number of rhythmic impulses in the spoken words.

From this they went on to painting pictures of themselves. They never encroached on the drawing space of another, they distorted the circle rather than disturb the others. They drew their hair, their 'pony-tails'. They could have achieved all this mutely, but they 'spoke', they wanted to explain themselves, to communicate, they supported their speech with gesture. Had one run the film through without sound one would have imagined them to be communicating with normal speech.

An intensive speech therapy reinforced the speech motivation of these children. Now, six years old, in a special class for those with central disorganisation of perception, these children are speaking, even if slowly, nevertheless intelligibly. The multi-sensory use of speech at an early age – and one cannot begin early enough – prepared the way for this.

In a mixed group of six to seven year old hearing-handicapped children with mild cerebral palsy, one child was particularly noticeable through her clumsy, awkward bearing. L. was seven years old, carried a large hearing aid on her chest, and was so sunken in on herself that she gave the impression of having an additional physical handicap. She could not sit cross-legged, made no contribution and did not speak. She nevertheless remained in the group – to the annoyance of a boy – and received the same challenges as the others. The boy, M., wanted to have nothing to do with her, refused to sit next to her or even to take over an instrument that she had just played. She became more and more awake and willing to take part with pleasure. She now wore a virtually invisible hearing aid on her ear. She clapped, moved and became less noticeable within the group. She then became noticeable once more through a good contribution on the xylophone in which she handled the beaters with particular skill. In about the tenth session she surprised us with a roll on the timpani, her beaters moving alternately quite quickly. The individual children were asked to play the timpani and as M., the boy mentioned above, had finished (he is described in example 7, p. 34), he spontaneously gave his beaters to L., remarkable! They were asked to play the timpani in any way they chose and the group was to react in movement. L. now played the timpani with mastery. With sure signals she led the children into stillness, to squatting, and enjoyed the way they reacted. With a further drum beat she brought them up again, and then she mimed a drum roll with her beaters all round the room. This fresh, upright, lively girl moved with assurance among a group consisting mainly of boys. She had so changed that one would not have recognised her external appearance. She expressed herself more often in vocal sounds and when it was her turn to tell a story on the African 'talking drum' for instance – this was an intuitive connection arrived at by the children – she talked at length and in great detail, though naturally we could not understand any of it. The other children noticed the change in her and M., who had previously regarded her with contempt, volunteered the unsolicited comment: "L. is really getting on, I wouldn't have believed it."

The blind and visually-handicapped

It is general knowledge that blind people have their compensation in their sense of hearing, that gives them access to the world around them. The tactile sense can be stimulated by the sense of hearing. Where the home environment is intact a blind child can have a well-developed sense of touch. In a bad home environment or with a child that lives in an institution and that does not receive enough attention the sense of touch will become blunted. A last access then exists through the sense of hearing.

The blind child is considerably isolated, he can, however, communicate well with music, that is, with the help of music and musical materials he can come into contact with other children.

In my examples I do not want to cite cases of blind children in general, nor give reports of children from such a devoted home background that their other senses had been fully developed and were therefore capable of acting as substitutes – in such cases, with training, a full kind of music making is possible. I would rather describe cases where in addition to being blind a further handicap was discovered, arising through the environment or from inside, and one case of an acquired visual handicap with considerable behavioural influence.

Because a blind girl, twenty months old at the time, found the sound of a drum worth exploring, she grasped the drum skin. Till then she had refused every hand contact. She only used her feet for touching. She touched the rails of her play pen, or her cot and every use of her hands for this purpose was rejected, whether active or passive. For this reason physiotherapy had not been successful for she reacted with lusty crying to every touch. When I saw Uschi for the first time she was like a small, drawn together parcel. Noticing that only the soles of her feet were active and touched things of their own accord I tried to establish contact by touching the soles of her feet and her legs myself, and it worked! She tolerated the beaters gently touching her soles, her legs, and along her thin thighs, using rhythms of different kinds, supported with some words, names and short verses. But she vehemently refused to take hold of those gentle beaters herself.

Several opportunities for touching were offered to her but she was never persuaded to hold anything in her hand. Small cymbals, played with a beater and held close to her ear were accepted with a mimetic reaction that increased to a smile. More and more her head would be lifted when she looked in the direction of a sound, slightly to the right or left according to its source (see pictures D). The eventual touching of the drum skin was sensational. She started with scratching movements and tapped it later with her palm. Then she groped for a small cymbal that was being played near to her hand, grasped it and then held her hand on it. The cymbal was now played in an even, quiet rhythm; for longer and longer she tolerated these vibration impulses and absorbed them with close attention. A little later she grasped the cymbal with both hands at the same time and kept her hands on it. In doing so she lifted her head every time and through the way she followed the movement with her breathing she made this experience visible.

The first time I saw her reach spontaneously for something was for a stick of jingles. Previously she had accompanied some lively music for recorder and xylophone by beating quietly on the floor with the jingle stick in correct time to the music. She then put the stick on one side; as the same music started up again she picked the stick up spontaneously and played with the music. She was able to distinguish musical differences in that she listened when a large recorder played slowly in long melodic arcs, but immediately clapped spontaneously when the small sopranino recorder started to play a more rhythmically accentuated piece. She responded in her own way to the contrast of this non-verbal challenge. She spoke not a word, however, and complied with practically no suggestions. "Dance, Uschi, dance" however – her song had become a dance – she understood at once and she smiled, showed pleasure, and sometimes joined in with clapping. The therapists provided her with a lively accompaniment.

Until now she had resisted standing in any way, had tensed herself and cried bitterly when one wanted her to do so. It was achieved in the end, however, with a large cymbal, held over her head and played loudly. In the undertow of sound from the cymbal Uschi was drawn upwards. She was first aware of the change of position that she had found so frightening when she was actually standing. Through the surprise of the moment she could not tense

An eight year old spastic boy at a bass metallophone.

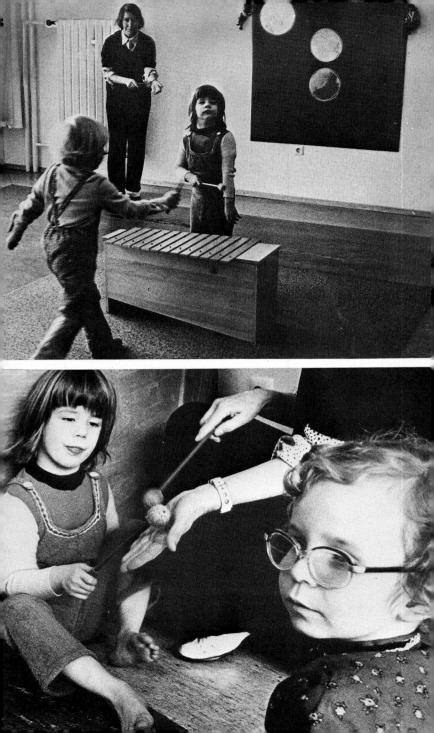

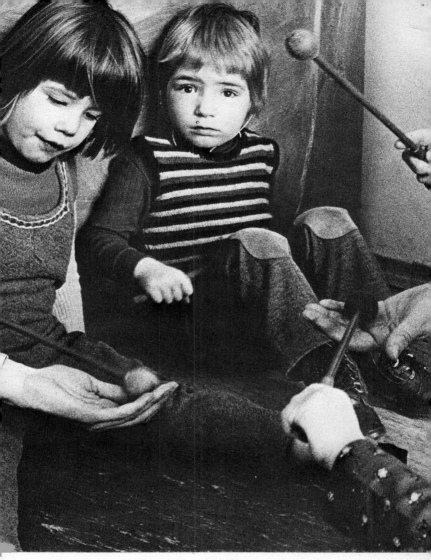

Left top: A group of children with impaired hearing experimenting at an instrument as part of a movement game.

Left below: Tatiana, with impaired hearing and an athetosis, has struck the instrument too vigorously. Now she is trying something more gentle on the therapist's hand.

Above: Striking the hand is now being tried by everyone.

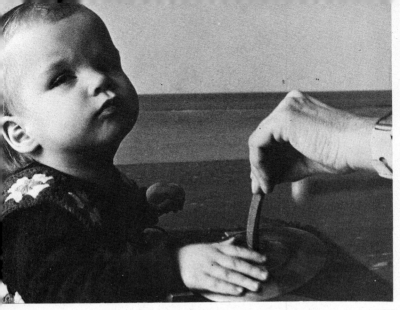

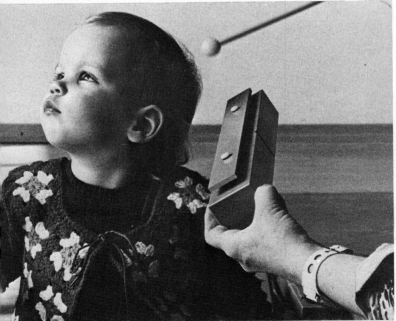

Top: Uschi, blind and nearly two years old (see case history p. 79 ff.) has her first experience of touching an instrument. For about two minutes she tolerates the vibrations of an even pulse on a small cymbal.

Bottom: Listening, she takes in the sound of a chime bar (resonator bell) after which she touches it.

Top: One of autistic Detlef's good moments. He has established eye contact and spontaneous physical contact with the therapist. He has taken part in a rhythmically spoken nursery rhyme with movement and some sounds (see case history p. 150f.)

Bottom: Now he is once more absorbed with himself, manipulating the claves in a stereotype, autistic way. He must be aroused with some new stimulus.

Left top: Four year old Renée listens to the recorder with full attention. A few sessions have made this possible (see case history p. 153). Renée is considerably retarded through severe deprivation and early brain damage. Through treatment it was possible gradually to bring her hands together. Her severe inner tension, that led to a diagnosis as a quadrispastic, has eased.

Left middle: She wants to touch the recorder but is not yet ready. She takes up a typical defensive attitude.

Left bottom: Now she makes contact with the object, an achievement brought about through affective contact with the recorder's sound.

Above: Renée now takes up the typical insulated pose of the autistic that she now shows less and less often.

Different ways of using a drum
Top: *In this group with disturbed behaviour the drum is used in an active,*
rhythmic way by a leader from within the group.
Bottom: *In this group of spastic children the drum is used as a support to verbal*
expression. Dependent on the sequence of the game the drums are exchanged, and
held communally so as to form a binding link that can be acoustic or non-acoustic.

Surprise use of the drum. By this means the therapist can once more bind together a group that has become dispersed.

Top: The group pictured earlier (H) are here playing together on instruments. Some children are watching the recorder that is this time keeping the piece together. The standing boy is hemiplegic. In the picture he is playing with both hands equally on the bass xylophone.

Bottom: The session that began with the drums and movement shown in H, ends with an ensemble of various instruments to which each child takes it in turn to move.

In a group of boys – with minimally impaired movement and mild behaviour disturbance – the drum serves as a means for visual and aural imitation at different levels.

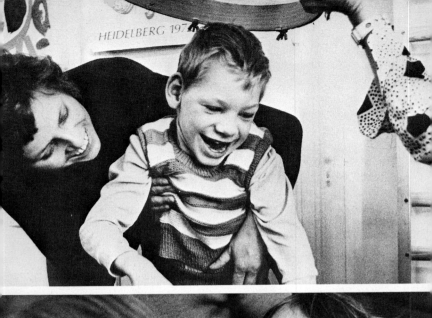

Top: Even children that are severely quadrispastic can experience pleasurable relaxation. R, who is blind and without speech, is here standing upright with the help of his mother. He was motivated to do this by the 'drum roof' held over his head.

Bottom: B. has tapped the drum that is held before the face of her playmate and is enjoying the effect (see page 91).

herself and her first reaction was to cry as she stood there. We kept trying this from time to time. After a while she stood for several seconds without crying. After some weeks she stood well, still held lightly, or holding herself up on a timpani, for instance. While standing she laid her hands on the timpani skin, tolerated the playing of the drum and felt the vibrations for many minutes. It was then possible with the help of beats on the timpani to get her to walk. One drum beat corresponded to one step, and with this stimulus she dared to take her first steps.

In these first attempts at walking she was offered various stopping places as a motivation. Lightly held by the therapist she walked in a large circle stopping at 'recorder playing', 'metallophone', 'triangle sound', 'jingles sound'. The sound source enticed her with its playing and she allowed herself to be enticed. Having arrived she then stood in front of the sound source and made little bouncing movements in time with the music. She often walked in this way from one stopping place to the next until finally she pressed forward so eagerly that she dragged the therapist who was holding her lightly on the hips, after her. It took a little while until she could stand alone and until she had enough sense of balance to be able to sway slightly from side to side as she was standing. Physiotherapy backed this achievement with relevant exercises.

In spite of this progress she seldom moved her hands. Yet when it was held out to her she took hold of the bigger recorder, which was as big as she was when she sat, with both hands. When holding the very small one she felt the holes. If one took it away from her and played it immediately she could connect the sound with the object. Something quite sensational happened not long ago: at first she touched the individual chime bars (resonator bells) that lay in front of her and beside her. She used her whole hand and individual fingers in alternation when the therapist played on the chime bars. If the therapist tried to lift any of them she actively pushed them down again onto the floor. After a quick piece of music on the high-pitched recorder that she particularly liked, Uschi lifted her head. Immediately she started moving in a way she never had before: she moved the left chime bar to the right, and the right to the left. She grasped these objects with delight and worked in this way for about two minutes. After this event she breathed deeply. In the following sessions she was similarly active after feeling the vibrations of the chime bars as they were played, but for a longer time, perhaps five minutes. She had grasped spontaneously with both hands for the first time. She produced some quiet humming for quite a long time; she sang a little; some speech was beginning to come. She can arrive quite unresponsive and revive in the session. She has a great need of sleep and is often ill. She is now two years and eight months.

A three-year-old girl, B., brought up in a children's home but now adopted, is blind, and in addition she suffers from an extreme restlessness and a fear of being alone – surely out of anxiety at possibly being abandoned again. She can move alone, she can speak, but finds it difficult to concentrate. She can hang on to a verse spoken in rhythm, however. She sings and speaks what she has heard again and again, it calms her. She accompanies herself by beating the small claves together. She listens intently and wants to be listened to. She demands total attention. Her blind partner, M., is quite the opposite. Shy, huddled together, M. has some damage to her hip – she plays for a long time with the gentle sounds of the metallophone. She is not seeking any contact, she is absorbed in herself. She cannot walk alone but she is able to stand. She reaches out to the cymbal held and played above her head. She stands for a longer period, for the first time. Here also the sound acts as a stimulus. She now calls B. with the metallophone and B. comes and sings her song with the claves while M. accompanies the song cautiously on her metallophone. For both of them the session has become one of encounter. There are also some attempts at speech. B. leads M. to the bass drum where they stand opposite one another and envelop one another in the warm, dark sound of this skin instrument. Blind B., who was formerly in an institution, talks at home about a 'blue' carpet. She is so excited and eager to come to the sessions that her mother sometimes takes a taxi so that the journey there, which usually takes an hour, shall not seem so long. To the misfortune of being blind she has the good fortune to have found such a mother, who has two other older children.

In the case of a boy who had acquired a visual handicap and extreme sensitivity to light – so-called 'Lyell Syndrome' – as the result of an infectious illness, music therapy brought about an improvement in behaviour in quite a short time. The real damage had grown in the course of the years into an extended one; sensitivity had turned into over-sensitivity. In spite of protection with almost black glasses – someone with normal vision would have seen nothing with them – the boy maintained a bent posture, his head no longer daring to look up with one or both hands always being held as a shield in front of his eyes.

Fabian came to our session on a bright, sunny, autumn day, in a bright, south-facing room at eleven o'clock in the morning. Not exactly favourable conditions for him. Shy of the light as he was he was placed against the light and the thin curtains were drawn together. The therapy plan was spontaneous: working against the boy's justified aversion towards brightness, to encourage feelings of inclination strong enough to make him act against his exaggerated behaviour, which had become characteristic.

With chime bars (resonator bells) an atmosphere of sound was created that enticed him to join in and play the chime bars that were offered to him. In order to see better he took off his glasses, but with his right hand he held his right eye continuously shut. Someone telling him to take his hand away had probably reinforced this behaviour. A musical challenge must bring about a change. The guitar provided a further stimulus. A therapist played chord combinations and soon allowed the boy to play the strings while she kept control of the fingerboard. In order to draw his attention to the process of changing chords and to the therapist's moving hand he was asked: "Say when you want a new sound." He asked for new sounds but did not yet look at the player's left hand. Crouched in a huddle Fabian played on the strings. The guitar was now being held vertically so that he would have to look up if he wanted to see the hand, but he didn't want to look up. Another purposeful suggestion was made to him: "Take this piece of wood and then you can make the chords brighter or darker (higher or lower in pitch), look, like this!" He didn't look but he heard all right. He also took the small rounded piece of wood and held it near his playing hand and rolled it up and down the fingerboard giving an effect of barré chords in glissando and he liked this. A further suggestion: "The guitar would like you to see what you are doing", moved him to look up. We now had a boy in a bright room, without his glasses, using both his hands and in addition looking upwards! Nothing was said, no praise was given, it was accepted as a matter of course. Every comment on his posture would have made him conscious of how unusual it was and he would have returned to that which had been usual until now. He went even beyond this situation himself in that he looked, even if only briefly, towards the bright window.

The second session, a week later, was one of those breakthroughs that seem sensational and unbelieveable.

Fabian came running into the room, his mother calling after him: "Don't you want your glasses?" He answered "No". He went at once to the bass xylophone and played it. He looked quickly at the boy Reinhard who was with him in the group and Reinhard asked him why he held his head on one side. I said to Reinhard: "You know that he doesn't see very well and that the light dazzles him." Nevertheless the visually handicapped Fabian was playing freely on the instrument with both hands. This stimulated the rather jealous Reinhard and he played this tune:

Bass xylophone

Fabian listened and copied it immediately and made free variations of the melody. Then he fetched a glockenspiel and, putting it on the broad end of the bass xylophone managed both instruments with his two hands. He struck all the bars accurately and if I spoke to him he looked at me raising his head slightly. He was interested in playing our drums that were hanging on the wall. The highest one he could only reach by stretching up, but he still held his head a little to one side. My suggestion "take two beaters and play the drum with both of them" caused him to stretch entirely with both hands and to look up. For the rest of this session he did not drop his head once, he ran round the room, reproduced a lifelike copy of a horse by quickly getting onto all fours, cantering around us and then, from the standing position jumping a long way, 1 metre, 42 centimetres. We measured it with his own height that he knew. The therapist then directed some more ensemble playing and he took the big triangle and played it and then put it on his head. This was a moment to offer him a tambour as a drum hat. He agreed immediately, "look, I'm balancing!" and he stood upright, with raised head and his hands stretched widely to the side. We showed this to his mother, and she said that he had so looked forward to coming again, and that this was already a gain if there was something at all that could give him pleasure. While he was active in the room the boy never noticed whether he was standing against the light or not. We had managed to create a situation whose attraction was strong enough for him to overcome his stereotype posture – from an original need it had subsequently become an adopted one – and this had allowed him to achieve what had seemed impossible. Outside the therapy sessions he now moves normally.

A blind girl with prenatal damage, already twelve years old, had not yet been to school nor been helped consistently in any other way. She had severely disturbed behaviour. She would come quite close to adults and children, feel them, and then grasp them by the neck (not an entirely harmless hold) and loved to fight with them. The therapy plan was consciously geared to distance. Only instruments were touched, drums that one held together with someone else, claves that one played reciprocally. The space was fully used and movement possibilities were offered. She was challenged from many sides and kept busy. Her first attempts at fighting were translated into movement. In the course of the session she no longer made her presence felt. She had a beautiful voice and remembered a tune at once. She spontaneously sang back a recorder melody that was played to her. She could always remember and repeat a song that she liked particularly, and as she sang it she swung herself higher and higher with each verse. She was classified as severely mentally handicapped, but in addition to melodies she remembered clapped rhythms at once. With such questions as: "How many legs has the stool on which you are sitting?" however, she would answer "three", "is the bass xylophone large or small?" she would say "small". The consistence of her wrong answers was amazing. But when asked: "How many sounds did you play?" she answered correctly "four". Although she had considerable contact with people she had little contact with things, and she would throw them around and would not touch them. She got used to the instruments, however, and after a few sessions she no longer threw them about. Her concentration improved, she walked freely in the room, or in some direction in response to a call, without the need to touch anyone else.

After the song 'There once was a mother and she had four children, the spring and the summer, the autumn and the winter',* the therapist improvised: "How do you feel about the winter, and about the summer?" The girl searched for a low-pitched, dark-sounding note on the bass xylophone and played it once, singing to it "the winter sound". Then she searched for a bright, high-pitched sound, and playing it several times, quickly and with accents, she sang to it "the summer sound".

Unexpectedly she would ask us: "What is wood like?" "What is metal like?" We had asked her such questions and now, with a cunning smile she was asking them of us.

We were able to play with a ball. She threw and caught it safely. With the rhythmically spoken words "ball, you, ball, me" a larger ball was so bounced on the floor that the partner could catch it easily. It bounced on the floor on the word 'ball', the therapist caught it on 'you' and the girl caught it on 'me' and so on. The therapist tried this with closed eyes, 'blind'. Through the regular rhythm she felt connected in a kind of harmony with the ball and the child.

In the course of a few sessions the girl became quieter and more secure. She accepted contact with things and she walked freely about the room. Her previous stereotyped wrong answers – they had become a convenient way of evading the issue – were replaced with real questions and correct answers.

---

* Orff-Schulwerk, *Lieder für die Schule*, II, No. 6. publ. Schott, Mainz.

Physical handicaps

Here we are mostly concerned with handicaps resulting from brain damage. They are clearly distinguished:

minimal cerebral palsy, is a slight physical disturbance, that shows itself in actions requiring movement co-ordination. It is so slight, however, that it is often mistaken for clumsiness, giddiness or lack of concentration,
hemiplegia, a paralysis, weakness or spasticity on only one side of the body,
quadriplegia, a paralysis, weakness or spasticity that includes arms and legs.

The physical handicap is accompanied by a delay in speech development. Mental handicap can, but does not have to be connected with it.

The spastic damage causes a deficiency of movement. Through motivation, released through sound, rhythm and play, movement that would otherwise be neglected can be brought into play. The will to move is important for a damaged movement function. This is where music therapy sees its task. Physiotherapy, remedial gymnastics and occupational therapy can build on the child's will to move.

Balancing exercises for minimal cerebral palsied children become meaningful when supported with sound. The child does not think of these exercises as being compulsory. When rhythmically supported, such exercises as kneeling on one knee, climbing onto a step and jumping down again, have a purpose and their repetition comes naturally from the rhythmic phrase. The play atmosphere created by the rhythmic or sound support does not make the effect less therapeutic, on the contrary it makes the therapy more effective. Moments of spasm that always arise in compulsory standing, walking or movement exercises, are moments of delay, that together with the accompanying negative emotional components are particularly inhibiting to development.

With hemiplegia one side is not fully developed and the child will always prefer to work with the healthy hand. If one reminds him that he should use the other hand he will mostly set up a conscious resistance. Using both hands must seem to be really necessary and he must practise their combined use. Spasms that may arise as a result are not harmful since the impulse to move compensates for them. For this reason corrections should not be made during this kind of activity.

With small children activities like crawling along tracks in the sand are possible, or playing with hoops or a ball making use of both hands. I find it beneficial when a child who is handicapped in this way can move with a mixed group, for he will then be more likely to overcome his difficulties. With older children a visual imitation game using both hands can be helpful, and it can be executed with or without an instrument used visually and acoustically. Imitation games on an instrument are equally helpful: at first the intervals need not be copied exactly, but freely, either with both beaters in an upward direction in pitch, i.e. to the right, with both beaters to the left, towards one another, away from one another, or with an alternating beat on the left and right side. In this play situation one should never stress the use of both sides too much. Working in co-operation with the physiotherapist is ideal, so that immediately after the music therapy the movement resources can be worked over.

One proceeds in a similar way in quadriplegic cases. A three-year-old boy had refused physiotherapy. He cried if one touched him, took hold of nothing spontaneously, and not at all with the left hand. He did not speak and could not sit without support. A recorder tune played especially for him made an enormous impression. He reached out and grasped the recorder taking it in his right hand. He could not quite manage the blowing. To help him to understand it a piece of paper was quickly brought and was kept aloft by blowing until it fell to the ground. It was also used like a fan and this fascinated him. The screaming and crying heard at the beginning of this session had vanished and never occurred again during the intensive three week treatment. He grasped the paper in his left hand (because he was holding the recorder in his right) and was able to hold on to it and fanned himself with it. We had won access to him!

Variations on this grasping movement were tried: reaching up high for the paper, taking a beater in the hand and exchanging the recorder and the beater. With the help of a second therapist who held him in a sitting position, he played with both beaters on a pair of bongo drums placed in front of him. In the following sessions he tolerated strangers in the room, something that had previously caused immediate screams; he had become emotionally more stable. Later he picked up the beaters of his own accord and tried playing the bongo drums with them. These two small drums, fastened together as one unit, are particularly appropriate for left-right playing. They are usually played with the hand, or with the fingers; for little Walter an intermediate stage with the beaters was necessary. His rhythm was taken up by the therapist and the way was prepared for a non-verbal dialogue and a partner relationship.

A further game was played with individual chime bars. Walter played eagerly and relatively powerfully and with extraordinarily loose wrists, and corrected the way he held the beaters for himself. His aversion to fur – he never touched a furry animal – an over sensitisation, vanished as if by chance: small blocks of wood covered with material or fur were thrown into a drum. By moving the drum from side to side they slipped about inside. He echoed this movement energetically with his own body. When invited he picked up the individual blocks, fur or not, and threw them into another drum. Finally he put them into a cupboard when asked to do so and did not hesitate to hold the fur-covered pieces in his hand. It was at this point that he first answered the question: "Which will you take now?" with "that one!" His hands were looser, they lay open and unclenched on the drum skin. The small cymbals interested him so much that he picked them up with both hands and with help struck them together. He played the big cymbal alternating with his left and right hand. He was so absorbed with his playing that he did not notice that for a long time he had been sitting without support!

From now on he sat in the sessions without support. He tolerated other people, looking at them and at other children carefully; he spoke, even if not very much, with understanding and was understandable. He still resisted standing, but held a hoop in front of himself and allowed himself to be pulled this way and that. By means of the hoop he then allowed himself to be raised gently and he stood for a while. He transferred experiences, so that, for instance, having learnt with the large cymbal that one could stop the sound by holding it, he did the same with the metallophone. He found touching things interesting and necessary – this is the best motivation. Within three weeks an anxious boy who trusted no one and who had no confidence in himself, had become a courageous boy, who could sit up alone, who had started to stand and walk, who tolerated others and made social contact with them and then spoke as well. His vocabulary increased; he had achieved the breakthrough to the outside world.

A similar breakthrough was experienced with an even more difficult case, quadrispastic, and additionally blind with organic speech problems. A boy whom one would rather have given up after having seen him for the first time with head drawn in, hands clenched, and at first producing no reaction at all. In a small group of severe spastic cases, all three or four years old, the boy improved to such an extent that he took part with his head held upright, and he raised himself further in that he was even able to reach upwards – so that he could reach the cymbal that was ringing and hanging over his head. He had refused to take objects in his hand and now he took a beater and played his drum with it. He showed pleasure, he touched the child next to him. The song 'Ringel, ringel Rosen, schöne Aprikosen' (Ring-a-ring of roses, lovely apricots) made such an impression on him that from then on he would eat raw fruit, which he had previously flatly refused to do. He eats now, still with help, but he does grasp his spoon. Even in hot weather he would arrive with very cold, clenched hands – he could not open the left one even with help. After about ten minutes in our music therapy they opened naturally themselves, even the left one; the blood supply had got to them and they were warm. Only the animation of being there and his inner participation in the session made this possible. His limited physical contribution of beating could not have brought this about.

Here we see the 'acoustic atmosphere', a totally captivating ambience of sound, combined with considerable speech stimulus, within which the children can vibrate. Here challenges are always being offered but in a fascinating way. The children loosen up, they make spontaneous movements that are otherwise impossible and through the music therapy they come to making relationships with one another.

This is the case in a session where the mothers are present and where they hold their children (see L, top picture). During the week they offer similar situations of stimulus, thus provoking exercises in movement in a spontaneous way. Communication between the mothers is also a help for them, something that does not occur in individual therapy.

Mental handicap

Mental handicap or retardation in mental development has many causes. 'Mental retardation' as the term already indicates, can be made up for to a certain extent, if its causes are external: such as too little attention in the early years, too few mental challenges, long stays in hospitals or children's homes. If the mental handicap has internal causes, then assistance in relation to the severity of the case, the use of resources and the intensity of the therapy is productive.

Mental handicap mostly brings about a bodily *clumsiness* and unwieldiness; fine motor activity has not been developed. This is accompanied to some extent by *hyperactive behaviour* and resultant restlessness – or on the other hand by a *listless inactivity* and general lack of interest. Walking often develops late and imperfectly. To this an *aggressive behaviour* or an *indiscriminate friendliness* can be added. *Retarded speech development* is always there together with a *deficient understanding of speech*.

Orff Music Therapy can help considerably in these cases. In confronting the abnormal behaviour that arises as a result of the mental handicap it can be effective in the following ways:

The *motor clumsiness* is tackled through the use of the instrumentarium. This is preceded by building up hand–eye co-ordination through visual imitation of gesture, and through visual use of the instruments. Various ways of striking the instruments, with the hands alone, with beaters, alternating right and left are tried.

91

To this movement exercises, for standing, walking, jumping, etc., supported by instruments that give the appropriate signals, are added.

The *hyperactivity* is tackled by making use of, including and working at the children's uncontrolled movements. Here one follows the child's lead. Quiet sounds, sung or hummed chords are also offered as sedatives, and with gesture imitation one tries to build up concentration. The tasks are changed as soon as the child loses interest but one tries to increase the span of concentration. One builds on small units and extends and lengthens these.

The *lack of drive for movement* is tackled through visual and acoustic stimulation. Visual stimulus would include the following of a movement or the movement of an object with the eyes. This is offered in an intensive way and is rich in contrasts, in order to touch the threshold of sensitivity, insistently but not obtrusively. Walking is stimulated by providing attractive objectives, there where the drum is standing, or following a resounding instrument.

The *indiscriminate friendliness* is tackled by offering a rich variety of activities, using the instruments as keepers of distance. Longer rhythmic sequences with clapping, walking, drumming provide a deflection from the self towards some other object.

The *retarded speech development* is brought on through stimulation of speech such as: calling through the drum, through the hand. Syllables provide the commands for walking, jumping etc. All speech utterances are accepted without correction, the children's words are seized upon and used and momentary situations are built into the therapeutic happenings. Appropriately significant gestures support syllables or words such as 'high, dark, behind', etc.

One confronts mental handicap with a rich musical offering, one changes the activities, one challenges the child. One also provokes the mentally handicapped child, one offers him artistically exacting, elemental art, not crumbs. One withdraws material that does not bring results, either because it is too difficult or not alluring enough. With the appropriate challenge one can stimulate interest. The mentally handicapped child needs incentive and lives on stimulation. Repetition is necessary but the tension of excitement must still be there.

With severe mental handicap where the children are inactive

and lethargic, it has proved beneficial to have one or two such children in a group that is less handicapped, or even a group of normal children. They do not disturb. If possible another therapist should be available to be at their disposal. The events in which they take part influence them but their reactions are very slow. Two or three sessions, that is two or three weeks later, fragments from previous sessions are given unsolicited utterance – a material upon which one can now build.

Example 1

A severely mentally handicapped seven-year-old boy, who sat without taking part in the activities of a nursery play group, developed an interest in the other children and for what was going on in his play group after spending four sessions – one a week – apparently taking no part in our music therapy sessions. He was with three normal children, one of whom was his brother. He looked forward very much to each session and in the third session he surprised us by repeating something we had done in the first session and then not repeated. He had previously tolerated no physical contact; now in a relaxed way he was leaning against his nursery teacher. His involvement with people and objects was beginning and was further encouraged in relation to this establishment of contact.

Example 2

A severely mentally handicapped boy with extremely disturbed behaviour developed himself into an integrated member of a group. At the beginning he only held his hands over his ears and emitted resistant groaning noises. He seemed almost unacceptable in this group and disturbed us exceedingly. Then he adopted a somewhat more friendly attitude to the therapist and allowed her to touch him. He was so resistant that he could hold nothing in his hand, but let it fall immediately, and one could have assumed muscular weakness. After a few sessions this same boy took a drum as he had often seen the others do, held it high, and walked round beating it almost triumphantly with powerful blows of his fist. At first he had been so resistant and anxious that he did not sit down; later he sat on the floor, and stood of his own accord, which cost him a considerable effort. If he was supposed to be playing an instrument he went to it with difficulty, dropped the beaters, but once seated behind it he began to play powerfully with rhythmically sure beats, and he accompanied a recorder melody with a smile that was both shame-faced and proud. He was so far attentive and ready that he entered into a game of question and answer on a xylophone, but only with the therapist. He gave up his groaning (see also A.K. p. 146).

Example 3

A four-year-old girl with a very low IQ, who moved in a heavy way and was troublesome and aggressive, seemed hardly acceptable in the small group in which we had placed her. She screamed pitifully, refused to co-operate in any way and in the first session only remained in her mother's lap away from the other children. Now, after some weeks she sits with the other children in the group, takes up suggestions, if often at first with a "no", plays rhythmically sure ostinato accompaniments on chime bars (resonator bells) and would not be conspicuous to any observer that came to look at the group. If one does not compel an at first protesting child to join in, he will come of his own accord after a while. As therapist one has to decide whether one can put up with him in the group, defer treating him, or give him individual therapy.

Most mentally handicapped children can manage a rhythmically organic sequence. It is also possible for them to make up melodies and remember these (see example 1, p. 28). Functional harmonies will not be managed without visual help. If the harmonic pattern repeats itself, a mentally retarded child of appropriate age can remember this as a repeated pattern. In the song 'Sur le pont d'Avignon' the tonic – the chord on the key note – and the dominant – the chord on the fifth degree of the scale, alternate regularly. Each chord sounds twice in each bar before the change occurs. In the eighth, the last bar, this pattern changes to one dominant, one tonic. It is easier for the child to learn a new pattern for the last two bars than to change the existing one. The seemingly complicated hand movement of crossing the left hand over the right will actually be a help to him:

The regular harmonic pattern of the Ennstaler Polka will nevertheless only be achieved by a child in a 'roundabout' way. He will find it difficult to do it in the 'simple' way (2nd example) and easier to do it in the complicated way (1st example), for he will be able to take that pattern in more easily.

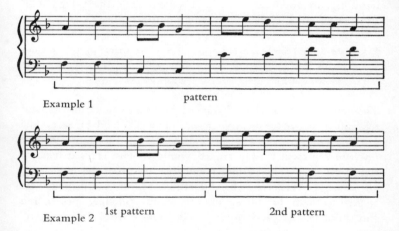

Rhythmic security and rhythmic co-ordination can nearly always be achieved. Nevertheless one should allow the children to give the pulse accent that seems natural to them. If one accepts it one has a satisfied child. In a group of ten mentally handicapped children all were clapping correctly in accompaniment to a recorder melody but in different time units, in crotchets (quarter notes), quavers (eighth notes) and in minims (half notes), also in syncopated patterns (see example 1, p. 28). It would probably have been difficult to have expected different specific rhythmic patterns from these children, but here they were offering them themselves. In developing this material one can work at each individual contribution, clapping them together one at a time, or bring them to particular attention in some other way. When musical variations occur through different personalities, they are more interesting, more productive and more alive. In addition, one should not always work within the same kind of structure with the mentally handicapped.

As therapist one must free oneself from expectations and fixed ideas – this is not easy – one must allow the child to have time for *his* decisions and not limit his time according to the therapist's ideas.

A ten-year-old girl, mentally handicapped and a chronic stutterer, hit the nail on the head with an unexpected answer. Quick as lightning, to our freely sung and spoken verse that ended with an open question, C. said "Nirgendwo" (nowhere).

Es geht der Schlaf beim Fenster herum
und der Schlummer beim Zaun.
Da fragt der Schlaf den Schlummer:
wo werden wir schlafen?

Sleep walks round by the windows
and slumber by the fence.
Says Sleep to Slumber:
Where shall we sleep?

The verse is meditative in character, the vowels predominate, and sch and m occur frequently (in German). The end of every line can be prolonged with a gesture of indication: with hands and arms one can represent a right-angled window, with crossed hands a fence. One has time to linger and thus promote the meditative character of the speech. The children echoed the words that were spoken to them, producing smooth, legato sounding speech, and this spontaneously and rhythmically spoken word "nirgendwo" was, as it were, the fruit.

With younger mentally handicapped children one does well to build on small units that can be put together into a larger form using linear co-ordination.

We can take a rhythmic verse as an example:

Säge, säge Holz entzwei,
kleine Stücke, grosse Stücke,
schni schna schni schna
schnucks!

Saw and saw the wood in two,
little pieces, bigger pieces,
zee, za, zee, za,
zux!

The therapist speaks the verse and makes an appropriate sawing movement that will surely be taken up by the children. The first task that has to be achieved is to stop the sawing movement on 'schnucks'.

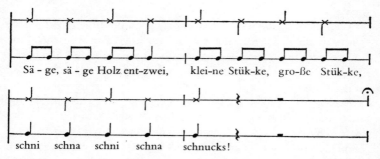

Sä – ge, sä – ge Holz ent–zwei,   klei–ne Stük–ke, gro–ße Stük–ke,

schni   schna   schni   schna   schnucks!

Since we are working with mentally handicapped children, who, if they can speak at all can often only speak slowly, we will need to speak the words twice as slowly once they have managed to say them at all. The sawing movement will now synchronise with the syllables, and the schni, schna will each last for two sawing movements.

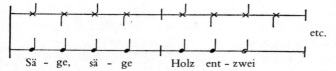

etc.

Sä – ge,   sä – ge   Holz   ent – zwei

With physically handicapped children the opposite might be necessary, a sawing movement every fourth or every second syllable according to the circumstances.

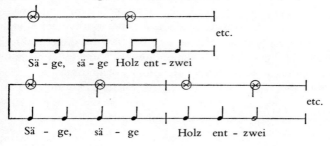

etc.

Sä – ge,   sä – ge Holz ent – zwei

etc.

Sä – ge,   sä – ge   Holz   ent – zwei

We can now notice where our arm is when we say 'schnucks' – close to or away from the body – why? We can then be conscious of where we start the movement: from far towards the body, or from close to away from the body, and we are requiring a decision to be made.

We can, according to capacity, play with the time units, bigger pieces or smaller pieces, faster or slower sawing movements. One can execute the sawing movements with a partner and here again decisions have to be made: to pull or to allow oneself to be pulled at the beginning.

Because the mentally handicapped child, and particularly the mongoloid, tends to repeat continuously and often has difficulty in coming to an end, the ending of our verse in the short formula schni, schna, schni, schna, schnucks is good in that it provides a clear ending. Each unit can be used as an ostinato, a repeated pattern:

kleine Stücke	little pieces
grosse Stücke	bigger pieces
säge säge	saw and saw and
schni schna	zee za

Each, spoken repeatedly, can become an ostinato to the whole. These are the beginnings of vertical co-ordination.

Finally we can make a scene out of it: A tree is dragged in and in imagination is laid on the ground. We decide who is going to do the sawing, and those who are looking on support the sawing movement with a spoken ostinato. One can also watch carefully while the sawing is taking place, is the piece thin or thick, etc. Should one child or a pair take an excessively long time over their sawing, one then has to distinguish whether they are doing so out of an incapacity for play or whether they are doing it for a joke. If a child shows his understanding of the game by doing the latter this should be correspondingly assessed diagnostically.

Work of this kind can be interrupted, one can continue in the next session, improve, co-ordinate, even make linear inter-connections, as long as the material still calls forth interest and is therefore usable.

Example 4

An extremely distractable, restless girl, but not of the worst kind, three years old, mentally retarded, diagnosed as possibly having autistic traits or alternatively with 'petit mal', could hardly be kept still in her place. Her handicap was too great for a movement sequence and no purposeful walking was possible. Like a moth she moved restlessly without aim, finally arriving by the window. In spite of this it was possible from the beginning of the session to lengthen her span of attention. In attempting this, however, she only reacted once to anything – the first time. With subsequent repetitions there was no reaction. This would suggest autistic behaviour. She was fascinated by a fully reverberating sound and gave full eye contact to the person who had made it. She was prepared to make some sounds on the drum but without any recognisable rhythm. In later sessions she held her hand for a long time on the bongo drum that the therapist was playing with her hands. She then placed both her hands on the two bongo skins. Another therapist played a recorder melody, and she took this in as if she were trying to learn it. She remained seated in her place. The recorder melody finished with a high trill – and this produced the first smile, that spread into cautious laughter. A trill played alone without the preceding melody did not have the same effect. She took no notice of it. An experimental comparison was made at the end of the session: a melody with a high trill at the end again aroused a distinct smile. It was the recognition of a form that produced a positive effect; a trill alone meant nothing.

The sound of the guitar held a great fascination for the child. In the second session it called her away from the window. Spontaneously she sat down and listened. She took hold of the resonance box. In the next session she showed the same fascination: she touched the strings, stroking them cautiously. The full attention she gave to this learning process could be read on her face. In contrast to previous sessions her interest in repeated activities was maintained without any turning aside. This refuted the previously suggested autistic behaviour. This otherwise mute girl began to make some vocal sounds that could now be built upon in speech therapy.

Older children with mental retardation often wander in their imagination and give an insight into their needs in the stories they tell. In this context music can become a releasing therapy for the playing out of anxieties, complexes or unresolved questions.

In one group session we were making thunder and lightning. One boy made an impressive roll on the timpani, he thundered loudly. He said: "Usually I'm afraid of thunder, but not now." At the therapist's suggestion that the thunder should come from further away he reacted marvellously. He said: "You make the lightning, I'll make the thunder." The lightning flashed . . . but no thunder came. Impatiently the therapist wanted to interfere thinking the child had forgotten the thunder. After about fifteen seconds, and that seemed long, there came a powerful thunder. "Now it's further away", he said. This was one of those healing and shaming moments for a therapist without faith. He stood perhaps two metres away from me, it was a small distance, but it sufficed for him to suggest a large distance in time.

Example 5

R., a five-year-old boy, mentally handicapped on account of brain damage, this condition having been reinforced through deprivation, was given individual therapy because he attacked other children. In the sessions he was suddenly violent, disruptive, almost evil, and at the same time tender, sensitive and gentle. He played sensitively on the metallophone and was prepared to play on it alternately with the therapist in a free conversation. He sang beautifully with pure intonation. Out of the contrast of 'out' and 'in' – one of his manias – he invented this melody and as he sang it he spread out and brought his hands together:

100

The boy presented this as a finished form. The way the melody comes to an end in the fourth and fifth bars (measures) is amazing, so too is the melody itself with its semitones.

After a few sessions it was possible to put him into a small group. He was only once aggressive with the material as he banged a recorder very violently on the floor. Finally he was in a hoop with the other three children. In the closest contact the four children turned round and round and laughed and R. did not make any aggressive use of the situation. He was so taken by surprise by this play situation that he perhaps even found it pleasing. From then on there were no more problems in being with adults or other children.

Example 6

A four-year-old girl, severely mentally retarded, without speech, with a stooping, shy posture, attained remarkable achievements on the chime bars (resonator bells). To her right a diatonic scale was prepared: C, D, E, F, G, A, Bb, C; to her left a row of lower pitched notes: C, D, F, G, A. The therapist made a start by playing a melodic phrase. When asked: "Did you like that?" she nodded. She played something similar. The therapist said: "I'll copy you, Evi" and Evi thanked her with a slight smile. She now made a start that was well structured and the therapist repeated it. She nodded. She remained within a narrow range of notes but always melodically recognisable, in a free organic rhythm. To the therapist's suggestion: "play one with a few more notes to it" she immediately offered a melodic phrase, a little longer and with more notes. Sometimes the therapist didn't repeat exactly but gave an answering phrase. The following kind of rhythmically flexible melodic lines arose:

She followed the suggestion that she should play the lower notes to her left. To the question, repeatedly asked: "Do you like that?"

she nodded every time. When the therapist played something to her on a triangle and asked: "Do you like that?" there came an unexpected shake of the head. This pleased the therapist for the previous confirmatory nods now had much more meaning. Always when single pitch sounds were made on triangle or claves, even when they were rhythmically shaped, she shook her head. She was better able to understand melodic form and this fascinated her. She accompanied a recorder melody with clapping, while a trill at the end of the melody thrilled her. As in the other case a trill played by itself gave no pleasure.

She held her head upright now, looking round roguishly. While being lightly held she stood up and walked to the bass drum or timpani. There she stood alone holding on fast to the drum, but it was possible to bring her to standing without support. In two sessions this was considerable progress. Melodic conversation on the instruments provided an affirmation that was particularly important for her, since she was without verbal language.

Disturbed behaviour

Behaviour disturbances take up a large part of the cases treated in music therapy. They form two categories: the one that shows *shyness, refusal to speak* and *resistance to contact*, and the other that expresses itself in *impudence, lack of consideration*, in *tantrums* and in generally *disruptive behaviour*.

Both attract attention in society, while the causes can have various origins.

The first kind is treated successfully in groups, the second mostly in individual therapy.

In all therapy the manner of approach is important, but in no cases so decisive as in those of disturbed behaviour. Here the success or the breakthrough will depend quite decisively on the therapeutic skill and potential of the adult. She must be particularly wakeful, ready at a moment's notice to be communicative and detached while of course remaining both inwardly and outwardly calm. It is no use thinking to herself that she has a certain number of sessions at her disposal, no, it is every moment that matters – in all therapy, but here particularly.

With aggressive cases the child will show the way, and a good resultant reaction is what matters: in withdrawn cases the therapist must activate a plan and react to the group situation. It is good to mix the over-anxious with those who are not anxious, as long as the latter are not aggressive. The anxious child may only come to the room with screams and will perhaps not come in at all without his mother. One lets the child sit by the door without pressing him to come in any further. He is sure to find what he sees and hears the other children doing irresistible, and if he doesn't succumb to it in the first session he will do at the beginning of the second session. With all the children that I have so far treated there was only one boy that stubbornly maintained his removed position for some time, feeling thoroughly secure with his mother. From this position he was with us inwardly and sometimes actively, until in the fourth session he was prepared to sit with us. He was a clever child who avoided every eye contact but looked at one continuously when one's attention was on the group. He was able to join in everything brilliantly, but he could stand no challenge. He got a tremendous kick out of having attention and not responding to it. When one demanded something of him, and this had to be done after some indulgent sessions, a wave of anxiety came over him, but by continuing to indulge him one was not helping him. He was fascinated by our group happenings. He was also very attracted to a gentle, six-year-old girl – he was just three himself. They were similar in their lack of contact with strangers and in their refusal to speak, being, however, lively at home where they almost ruled their families. In contrast to the boy the girl was co-operative from the very first session, and in spite of her over-anxiety she even gave an occasional answer. The boy was just as fascinated but he was not going to let on to himself or to us that he was. Now, a certain spell has been broken with them both and it is worth noting that there there is now a spontaneous verbal response to challenges. Two other children have joined the group: a boy – five years old, is small in stature with a cardiac disorder, not able to take any physical strain. He is over-intellectual, speaks when he wants to, asks irrelevant questions and is, through his egocentricity, emotionally limited and socially unresponsive. The sound of the instruments overwhelms him, he becomes expansive and gives attention.

The girl, now four and a half, came when she was three and a half to therapy sessions and is described in her previous condition later on. Now, in this that is for her a new group, she is the strongest, she smiles, speaks, sings and plays with confidence. The new group has brought about no setback for her.

The things that happen in the group have a levelling effect in a positive sense on the individuals. They prune excesses and supply deficiencies. The same challenge and the same occurrence has a different effect on each participant, what is missing is replenished. The heterogeneous nature of a group can be conducive to this.

A further example of a heterogeneous group (see J, bottom picture) A three-and-a-half-year-old girl, the youngest in the group, was excessively shy, spoke not a word and was at first always crying, though she did suppress this for she liked the session. In the first session she could not manage without her mother's presence. She then came more and more out of herself, and under her shell of shyness quite a strong-willed little person could be seen, who in the end could shake one firmly by the hand. She then trusted herself to speak, even more to sing. She played the instruments choosing first the smallest, later the largest. She played powerfully, skilfully and decisively. Well-supported at home, her behaviour improved considerably.

She was in a group with a girl who was already seven, physically very labile, who at school would cry at the slightest request or even when someone just spoke to her. She had lost her mother at an early age, and in spite of a good second mother she had never got over this shock. She was interested in the movement games and in playing the instruments from the first moment. She came to the first session a sad little girl and left it with shining eyes. From time to time she came more out of herself, made some suggestions of her own accord and was very co-operative. After ten sessions she could be discharged as *improved*.

A boy in this group, strong and healthy, was exceptionally shy and retiring with strangers. In the sessions he had no confidence and liked to hide. He responded to challenges, played when he wanted to and then over-loud and energetically. He often lay on the floor behind his instrument. That he was allowed to do this without correction and that the therapist was actually interested in his devious ideas, soon made him less conspicuous, and he came more and more into the general direction of the group. According to his mother his behaviour had improved, he was more responsive, and his change of behaviour had been noticed by acquaintances.

Another boy in this group did not know what to do with his excessive energy. He had the will to be co-operative but with his untamed and exuberant character he was often unable to achieve it. His loud and vigorous beating of the drum, his screamlike calls were tolerated by us, the therapist even stimulated them for the whole group. He was equally enthralled by very quiet sounds. Between these extremes a controlled, medium-loud level of sound had to be found. We see him in the picture playing his chime bars (resonator bells) in an appropriate way. (J, bottom picture).

The third boy in the group suffered from hemiplegia. He had as good as lost his autistic traits. He had been in another group for a year and had been occupied almost exclusively with his own ideas. *One* particular rhythm interested him and he would become absorbed in it in a stereotype way. Gradually he took more notice of his surroundings and in this present group he is now very acceptable. In the picture he is only using his left hand; in other pictures of the group he plays with both hands.

The fourth boy, over-eager, pushing himself forward, has to learn to get on with others and to accept other people's ideas. We see him in the picture as leader with the drum, absolutely in his element. He has a remarkable memory for all that goes on and for every nuance, but quite as remarkable was his inability to produce the sounds himself. He would confirm this himself "but my instrument isn't sounding!" In the meantime he has become more sensitive.

In this group we had combined shy, over-eager, and excessively loud children. The challenges in movement and play soon brought them together into a small ensemble in which each had his own task, but was linked to the others as part of a whole task. No solo exercises were expected from individuals and they were linked from the beginning in an integrated play and grew together in this way. The therapist was flexible and the group went with her in both productive and digressive situations. The flow was not interrupted; it regulated itself through the play situation.

105

Example of older disturbed children in a school situation

It was possible to interest a class of fifteen to sixteen year old children with disturbed behaviour – a so-called EMR class (educationally and mentally retarded) in a California High School in a gramophone record, since the therapist had broken them in in their first session. A piece from Orff-Schulwerk was played (Murray, IV, p. 46, No. 3) from the Harmonia Mundi Musica Poetica series. Both boys and girls liked it and wanted to hear it again. A boy tried to play the melody on an alto xylophone. It was the second session with this class.

It was especially this boy who had been so intolerable in the first session. No word of the teacher's was left without comment. His remarks made the others laugh; he had to be the centre of attraction and not I. He had to be won over! I suddenly asked: "Have you ever made a telephone call to Europe?" This question was accepted and gave me a chance. I told them of my call the previous evening.

We now developed an overseas call with various roles: the two people who were talking to one another, the operator, with amplifier, satellite, etc. I suggested quite openly to the boy who had been causing trouble with his irrelevant comments: "Why don't we have you on an island in the middle of the ocean? All calls would have to go through you, and you could contribute to every conversation." He fulfilled this role superbly. He stood in the middle of the room and had a key position. The conversations of the class were appropriately spicy. At the end of the session he wanted to help me. In the second session he soon learnt the xylophone melody, he was so keen. Now each one was given a part in the piece. To the most hostile of the girls I gave the triangle with only one sound but at an important place, and I said to her: "You must stand up when you play, your note is important." Her reaction was unexpected: "I'm important, I'm important!" she said. The piece was soon satisfactorily interpreted and then compared with the record. This interpretation raised the whole atmosphere of the class and their general behaviour improved.

A large, fat boy in this class was conspicuous through his obscene and cheeky talk. By chance, in the collected sayings of Carl Sandburg *Good morning, America*, I found something that would apply to him.

Each child read one of the sayings that I had collected together followed by a recurring refrain: "There are damm' lies, lies and statistics". Apart from the fact that he could not read very well why did he hesitate? What had happened? The boy who let far worse words trip easily off his tongue stumbled over such a printed word as "damm'". It was like a punishment for him to have to read the word aloud in public. Unfortunately I was only working with this class for a short time as a guest, but of the four sessions each one became better. The block of resistance in the class became less rigid and more transparent so that one was aware of its individual components. The co-operative ones soon got the upper hand and in general everyone became quieter and more tolerable to one another. The teachers of this class confirmed that this behaviour had transferred itself to their other lessons.

We have effective musical forms for building the kind of integrated behaviour that is desirable within a group:

1. Rondo form, with individual solo episodes
2. Imitation form

They also provide a means for binding a group of disturbed people together, and they make it possible for a musical happening that is non-directive and non-verbal to be maintained through its own momentum.

1. Rondo form that binds together in ensemble playing, promotes musical integration. One plays with the others, as an individual one helps to shape the piece, one begins and ends together. As one plays one adjusts to a certain volume of sound and one comes away from 'me' and comes nearer to 'us'. To bring about any integrated play at all the therapist cannot start from an aesthetic point of view. She must tolerate playing that is too loud from one or more, and overlook also the clumsiness or frustrations of the shy, that is to say she sees it without comment. She must encourage or check the *energetic* impulse. It is up to her to do this in such a way that the individual unconsciously accepts it.

Social integration comes as secondary and important element in the musical integration of a rhythm and sound ensemble. It is partly prepared in the preliminary musical integration in which the individual solo episodes contribute particularly. An individual plays in the so-called B part, and he forms his own contribution instinctively in relation to the combined tutti or A part. He has to decide, for he is not confined to a particular rhythmic length or to particular notes. Of course with prepared material every creative act needs constraints so that the act of choosing does not use up all the creative energy. Free play for the individual involves an adaptation to the whole; for the group it means accepting, enduring, tolerating the individual contribution. Social perception can be developed step-wise in this way. One will find it more difficult, the other easier. Above all every comment or drawing attention to particular points will disrupt the unconscious absorption of such a situation.

2. In imitation an unconscious absorption also takes place. One observes a gesture, for instance, and copies it. One stands alone, the group opposite him. The group imitates as if they were looking in a mirror. The imitation of a gesture occurs in silence, one submits to the other's gesture, one fulfils it. One takes on "the characteristics of another"* – an extremely important social moment – one assimilates them. The individual contribution will show the individual character, and it will be taken up, accepted. The therapist should start and she should see that the whole occurs in silence. Ingenious, comic gestures should not be received with loud laughter but with silent understanding. One should aim at an organic movement sequence.

With instrumental imitation a sound can be imitated only visually, and therefore silently, or the reverse can happen. (Here, too, we are not aiming for a correct, exact rhythmic-melodic imitation at first, our considerations are not primarily musical.) One single beat on a drum carried out in silent imitation has a tremendously effective power. All this should be absorbed unconsciously and worked at. A social climate arises. Every family has its own climate in which a child grows up, and its own fertile soil that fashions and affects a child in a favourable or unfavourable way. A group therapy session produces a specific climate and this affects a child. Remarks

* Nitschke, A.: *Das verwaiste Kind der Natur*, Max Niemeyer Verlag, Tübingen, 1967.

and commentary should encourage this climate, inept talk disturbs and destroys it.

These two examples of forms should show how closely connected musical activity and the practice of social experience can be. The result may even be aesthetically satisfying, but the starting point is quite different from aesthetic.

The members of a group with behaviour disturbance may be very different from one another but their problems are similar. As therapist one must allow every individual their own characteristics and help to stabilise them. One should not make a meek, good child out of a lively one, nor a cheeky one out of a shy one. Each should be measured according to his size and led accordingly, to exist in his way with others, but also to understand others.

Children whose behaviour is so disturbed that they cannot tolerate other children and attack them – out of over-sensitivity or jealousy, whatever the reasons may be – are given individual therapy. The aggression, the swearing, the active attacking, these a child acquires from his environment. Directly, because he has seen and heard such things, indirectly in defence of his own person.

A new environment, a new climate can already be a help in itself. When aids such as instruments are added to this, then most cases can be helped. The instrument has more than one function:

1. It has a distancing function, it stands between therapist and child.
2. It has a communicative function, it provides an understanding of a non-verbal kind.
3. It has an integrative function, it connects therapist and child.

In my experience individual therapy is most effectively carried out with two or even three therapists together. One therapist then take the lead, taking the session in one direction or another. The others are co-operative, helping the child as indicated to them, or simply helping to bring about a group happening. The child feels more free, not so much the centre of attention as in the one-to-one situation. For the therapist it is good that she can talk to her colleagues about the child and that more than one pair of eyes and ears are observing him.

If the behaviour disturbance is due to severe brain damage, or conditioned by early childhood schizophrenia, then, for the time being, an active music therapy, even in the broadest sense, is often impossible to carry through and is correspondingly ineffective. If a child, for example, has no feeling for his environment, can handle no objects, throws himself onto an instrument, climbs onto it or cannot take in its sound at all, then a pre-therapy has to be undertaken. Being calmed by the effects of shaded light, colours, water if he tolerates it, also currents of air, scent, soft material perhaps. Listening to music can also have an 'influence'. If the effects of such treatment are monitored by EEG equipment, a point of access may perhaps be found. The more difficult the case the more individual it will be. One must proceed from case to case with a particular personal commitment and feel where positive access, where interest, perhaps fascination can be achieved. If the child is musically gifted – and there are differences here – access is made easier.

Examples of individual therapy

A seven-year-old boy whose behaviour in school was intolerable came to music therapy. Slight brain damage and his home environment had made an aggressive youngster out of him. He kicked people in the shins, threw them down, broke his toys, shouted a lot, used swearwords etc.

On the first occasion he charged into the room making straight for the timpani and played it at once loudly. "Am I allowed to play it as loudly as I like?" "Yes". "And if it gets broken?" During these rather loud bangings the therapist could only wish that it would not be broken, not because of the damage, but that the boy's trial of strength should meet with some resistance. The therapist also knew that for such a trial of strength there were perhaps other materials that would be more suitable, and she wished that her dream of an ideal therapy unit were already realised: a large room in the centre with various side rooms, one with painting material, one with solid hard things, one with water and various kinds of syringe, one with shaded lights and cushions to lie on . . . But she had to help herself with things as they were and she noticed that W. was offering good rhythms, one sound with the left hand and two with the right, this continuously for a long time and then he came to

110

this regular rhythm:

The boy found the bass xylophone, "will it break?" He also tried the soprano xylophone and that stood there ready for him to choose. Breathlessly he went to all the instruments in an excited state. He followed no suggestions, his nervous, hectic behaviour precluded listening. He fetched several instruments and placed them all round him playing them relatively skilfully like a percussion player. He glowed and said: "That sounds full and loud!" At that moment he was not talking about breaking things and in this way the first session came to an end.

In the following sessions he explored everything that he could see. He asked: "May I?" and took two hoops from the wall. He was not unskilful in the way he handled things but his span of concentration was very short. Already in the second session he asked if we could play together. He took the small cymbals, the therapists taking recorder and bongo drums. We improvised. He next took off all the notes of the bass xylophone and acceded to the request to use both hands when doing this. He then played on it from within the resonance boxes. He also wanted to unscrew the timpani and take it apart. Again the therapist thought of her ideal room with an instrument workshop. We were then able to convince him of something, that inside the the bongo drums there was 'nothing' and that one needed this space in order to be able to produce the sound. So far the boy had been excellent, interested, admittedly also destructively, though only in order to discover the technical structure of an instrument. He came very willingly and would have liked to stay longer.

The following game resulted from his stereotype talk of breaking things: his (red) beaters say: "The instrument gets broken", the beaters play the word phrase, repeating it and getting louder. Soon he changes to the words: "I'll break everything up". The blue beaters of one of the therapists ask "why?". The white ones of the other therapists "I'll make it whole again". With his vigorous playing one of the bars falls off, he allows me to put it back. He is

111

then interested in ensemble playing, later he listens rather longer than usual to the sound of a cymbal and becomes quieter.

In a later session the beaters speak again: "I'll break everything up". The therapist tries by changing the rhythm to make this stereotype sentence into something of a game:

I'll break it up to - day!

I'll break it up, I'll break it up, I'll break it up to - day!

He accepts this and goes along with it.

But there was more to come. When in the next session he started up once more with "I'll break it up today", the therapist did not structure it for him this time and the white and blue beaters were silent. She let the boy have his head. He started at once on destruction. He took the bars off the bass xylophone and threw them on the floor. The therapist talked about "salad"★ which amused the boy no end. The therapist brought a large, strong sheet of paper that he could tear. Stretched over an upturned drum he beat upon it until it was torn. Not even this diversion was enough for him. He now threw the bars of two other xylophones about and trod on them with his feet. The situation was getting dangerous. It was forbidden to throw the bars out of the window. The words "instrument salad" took him somewhat aback. As the second therapist said: "you could put the salad into a bowl" he was really rather relieved at this way out. The resonance boxes were the bowl and somehow the bars were put inside. With this the session was at an end and he went out satisfied.

On the next day he accepted all suggestions willingly. He accepted them as being a help. At the instrument the beaters again said: "I'll break it up today". The white beaters said: "Not now, not now!" He entered into the spirit of this. As he wanted to take the notes off again it was explained to him how long it had taken us to

★ "salad" in this context means nothing in English, but in German it is an expression for "what a mess!" while still meaning "salad".

put everything to rights the day before. This he was able to understand.

There was a game with thunder and lightning and rain. He decided the order and which instruments should be used – "that will be the lightning". The empty resonance box he knew well and it seemed good to him for the thunder sound. He said: "Shall we take the bars off?" "Of course!" He made a good thunder in the resonance box. The nervous twitches that he had always had at the beginning of an activity were not noticeable today.

In the next session he took the hoop, spun it and let it run down of itself and stepped onto it, not aggressively but to test his skill. A movement session grew out of this with jumping as the theme. From white carpet square to white, from red to red, there were different ways of using the available material. The boy who had previously said "I'll break it all up" was now jumping over the instruments, and if one seemed too high he would jump alongside in order not to knock it over. Skilful as his hands were, his feet and legs were clumsy. Movement-wise there was still much that could be done.

The time of his stay had come to an end. In music therapy he had never once used swear words, never screamed with rage. His early, entirely egocentric behaviour had developed into good social behaviour. He kept the rules of a game and he made rules himself that he also kept. After the breakthrough with his need to be disruptive he became quieter and more co-operative.

There are children that appeal to one particularly. Although the therapist should be able inconspicuously to give each child a good measure of affection, there are nevertheless individual children that move one especially. It is not those children that one takes a liking to immediately, but often those with whom it is difficult at first to establish contact.

Such a one was Ralph, aged seven years. A good looking boy, well-formed, he wandered into the room with sunken head. He went to the prepared timpani. He looked into the round circle of the skin. The therapist said: "It's like a mirror". He answered: "Yes, but one cannot see oneself". He said this very slowly but very beautifully. For the first and only time he said; "I am Bambi". Since the

113

therapist then introduced herself and the second therapist by name and pronounced the boy's name, he never went back to his pseudonym. The names of the instruments pleased him and he spoke them in a meaningful way. He sought eye contact but granted it only surreptitiously. Sitting at the metallophone he asked for a song about 'Martin',* – later, it was now Christmas, 'Ihr Kinderlein kommet',** (It is worth noting that shortly before this he had said repeatedly to the psychologist: "All children should be dead.") He asked: "Play it again" and played with me. To the question who should begin he made the decision. He relaxed and one sensed his inner joy. As he was identifying himself too much with a drum the therapist tried to give him a sense of reality. With words like 'one, two, three, four, five, we are at your side' and others arising out of the situation one could bring him back out of his self-absorption. Such words thrown in quickly are effective; they do not tear the boy away from his game but draw others into it.

In further sessions his sensitivity was noticeable; he remembered and wanted to repeat things. In ensemble playing he reacted well. At first the stimulation of the therapists was enough for him to become absorbed. Now he stopped when they stopped, became louder, quieter, faster, slower. He made comments in conspicuously beautiful language.

His case notes that could now be seen for the first time spoke of severely disturbed behaviour, conditioned by the brain, with considerable aggression, with mental retardation and disordered speech.

The guitar was a good contact instrument. The player fingered the chords herself, the child stroked the strings. Various chord combinations were played. The child identified himself with the sound and slipped once more into himself, as it were. The therapist therefore fixed the chords: "That is my chord, this is your chord, and that is her chord". Not at once, but soon, he was able to or he wanted to be able to distinguish the various chords. As my chord came he gave me a profound look and said: "Your chord". To make a joke the player played the open strings. At this Ralph

* Martinmas (11th Nov.) There are German folk songs about St. Martin.
** A Christmas carol.

looked up. We began our game: when the open strings sounded we knocked on the resonance box and said: "Chords, guitar, please!" and the guitar played the three chords once more. Ralph named them and thus a good social relationship was unobtrusively developed between us. Ever more playfully did he say the "Chords, guitar, please!" in his beautiful, sonorous voice.

Subsequently he asked for hiking songs that he knew from records. He gave us the title but unfortunately we therapists were not very secure with the words. He did not help us as yet though I am sure he knew them. In a later session he sang several songs fairly loudly, but still intimately, and with faultless texts. He didn't repeat them, however. For him the proper time for singing had past and he didn't want the same thing twice. But he never entered into any of the songs we did – yes he did: Runda, Runda, Runda, Rundadinella,★ a song without text except for the syllables pleased him. From now on he always wanted to hear this and then sang it with us. He made up his own text:

Runda, Runda, Runda,
der helle Tag ist da.
(the bright day is here)

This was remarkable for this reserved, overshadowed boy. Later as an alternative second line we had

Runda, Runda, Runda,
die dunkle Nacht ist da.
(the dark night is here).

He sang it repeatedly and accompanied himself on the tiny cymbals, that he took with him at the end of the session – it was a Friday.

At the next session on Monday – he was having five weeks in-patient treatment in which he was being given a thorough exposure to behaviour therapy – he walked in with the two cymbals as if he had only just walked out. He wanted 'Runda'. So that it did not become too stereotyped we tried to interest him in playing instruments. He suddenly asked: "What is an instrument?" We explained

★ Orff-Schulwerk, *Music for Children*, III, Schott & Co.

and he repeated the explanation after us. He was particularly impressed by the resonance and what the resonance could bring about. As the therapist said carelessly: "The kind rubber is useful to us" (it is stretched along the resonance box and serves as a support for the wooden bars) he asked suddenly: "Why did you say kind?" The therapist now had to explain this and from now on be more circumspect in her choice of words. Some rather majestic, declamatory sentences, either from poetry, or improvised, were now spoken into the good resonance of the room. These were alternated with faster sentences, spoken into the room as before, but entirely improvised and arising out of the situation. This was to provide a contrast and to prevent a total loss of reality. It was like a stage rehearsal for a play where the comments of the producer interrupt the flow of the action. Ralph entered into the spirit of this very well.

He came more and more into a dialogue relationship with the therapists, he no longer 'lost' himself, he was aware of relationships with individuals, took up suggestions and gave us some.

When this child left us it seemed like the departure of a friend to the therapists. He had had ten sessions of music therapy. For him as for the therapists they had been harmonious; they represented a constructive moment in his life. We had not seen the boy described in his notes – disturbed behaviour, aggressive, disordered speech.

Autism

Autism reveals itself through disturbed behaviour. It is a disturbance in the general attitude to the environment, in the balance between the inner and the outer world, a disturbance of the exchange, the projection from the inner to the outer and from the outer to the inner, the process of for and against one another, the taking in and the giving out. The autistic person is isolated through his incapacity to make communicative relationships. It can have various origins and can take various degrees of severity. It is partly the result of a disturbance of brain function and partly the result of an unsuitable environment.

For the autistic person the relationship to the mobility of the organic world is disturbed, he has no interest in the exploration of material. To him a thing is a thing that he will turn in a stereotype, purposeless way, or on which he knocks in a purposeless way. He favours small, often transparent things. Knocking rhythmically is an activity with purpose, creative, within the framework of a rhythmic idea or phrase. When the autistic child knocks he is not exploring, he is unanimated, in fact stereotype. He lacks the sense of a relationship to anything else, to the idea of changing it or forming it in any way. He is afraid of every change. He wants to stay where he is, not to start anything, not to touch anything; he seems to want to remain in the middle of a situation without beginning or end. He remains within himself, rejects all contact, has no relation to persons or objects. His sense of perception seems to be absent. One often sees, however, that they do perceive, and notice, even sensitively and in great detail, and that they very quickly shut their 'contact lens' once more so that they do not react. They behave as if they had seen, heard or understood nothing. If this behaviour is practised for a long time it gives rise to a condition out of which the autisitic child will not find his way. The older the child that displays autistic behaviour is, the more set and unpractised are his possibilities for reaction.

The treatment that an autistic child receives from his environment often corresponds to his behaviour. One stops speaking to him or stimulating him because he doesn't react. This results in a hardening of his behaviour. Speech is not developed although the capacity to speak and understand speech is there. Because of his unreacting behaviour and the resulting reduction of stimulus from his environment, he doesn't acquire the necessary education for what is, in some circumstances, a normal disposition. It is a vicious circle. He is classified as mentally handicapped because of his behaviour, but he is not. He lives as if behind a window, he camouflages himself, protects himself, but he does perceive or he would not be able to put up his defences so promptly. More severe and milder cases can be distinguished from one another. The appearance of autistic traits occurs mostly at three or six years old. In his third year the child has become aware of himself and has started to set his will, here inactive, against his environment; in his sixth year school presents challenges to which he is not yet equal or which he is unwilling to accept, and he is over-taxed through what is expected of him. The family often make demands of their good and gifted child too early and too frequently. His autistic behaviour is a defence, an appeal to the environment, a protection phobia – he reacts no more.

Into this codified being, closed and locked, we have to try to penetrate. Trying to unlock with the wrong key stiffens resistance. Although autistic children often behave in the same way, this is not to say that they do so for the same reasons, or that their basic attitudes and dispositions are the same – they cannot all be unlocked with the same key. If one succeeds in finding one key – to multiply it is useless. The autistic child demands the most individual of treatment. That is why we know so little about him. If we want to penetrate and stimulate a reaction from this being we must get very close and actually do the same as he is. What is he doing?

I saw a ten-year-old boy, at this time severely mentally and emotionally disturbed, without speech and certainly without understanding of speech. It was said that his environment had brought it about. It was impossible to prove if a tendency to a mental handicap were present, but it was known that as a child he had been abandoned by his parents for whom he was inadequate, and through his behaviour more and more so.Where there is no challenge there is no reaction, development is stunted. In the home where he now lives he is housed in one room with mentally handicapped children of the severest kind. One of them is always screaming out of some need or other. As one comes into the room one's greatest desire is to leave it again as quickly as possible. The boy I want to describe was standing by a rail – the mirror on the wall behind reminded one of a ballet practice room – he was making stereotype movements with the upper half of his body, forwards and backwards. Did he see himself in the mirror? He had pulled his hair out on one side and it looked terrible. He was otherwise good looking on the side where he had fair hair. He rocked to and fro and I went and made the same movements opposite him without looking at him. I did not try to get eye contact. He noticed what I was doing and stopped moving. I stopped too. He started again and so did I. This went on for about ten minutes. Then he stopped altogether and went into a corner and I went too, quietly, inconspicuously, and we established a movement relationship here. The boy executed a small jump. I did the same. Gradually his face relaxed and showed pleasure. Nearly half an hour had passed, one could say, in a communicative relationship. As he noticed that I was going again his face looked sad. The contact at his level, doing something with someone else had made him happy, the end of this contact, sad. He had felt both emotions and had shown that he felt them.

By observing the tiniest indications and by holding oneself ready to be led, the therapist can perhaps reach the innermost locked door, often after a long journey there, where the child himself has lost the key. We come with the child deeper into his world and can then take him out again with us.

What can music do? At first very little, for the autistic child often rejects all sound, it is foreign to him, it does not change him. A tactile movement that stimulates the senses is also foreign, his stereotype knocking is done with the back, the rejecting side of the hand. If one succeeds in turning this movement round so that he touches something with the inside of the hand, even if only once as a final cadence, one has achieved much. With the boy described above it was possible to bring the rocking and jumping together in relation to one another and, through alternating them into a form. One had thus interrupted their stereotype nature and, by including the second kind of movement, had made an approach to object confrontation. Every approach towards something, even if it is only towards a movement, is already an object experience or a preparation for it. The prefix 'ob' in Latin means: 'towards', also 'for the sake of something'. Thus it is a preliminary stage to *contra,* which means 'to give conscious opposition', which one can only do when one has established one's own position. The autistic child does not present his 'contra', he remains neutral.

The boy described above is a case of the most severe autistic damage, weighed down by the years of inactivity and unprocessed environment stimulus. With much patient attention a more human condition could be achieved. The rubble of time had perhaps already crushed the seed within this child, and he was suffocated under this burden.

The earlier one tries to bring out the autistic child's personality with patient attention, the more likely will one's intention succeed.

The minutest indications should lead one on. Autistic children like to spin a thread in the real sense of the word. This meets their sensibilities half way; a thread is the most unmaterial thing possible; it is at the boundary of the visible. It was a nylon thread that brought one boy into contact with a group.

He had pulled it out of a nylon carpet. All the others – six children aged five and six years – were involved in a happening. Christof pulled at his thread and looked at it. In the previous sessions he had always kept apart and was preoccupied with himself. It is possible that in his own room he repeated the activities that he had seen downstairs. He was clever, asked questions, but often devious ones. As he looked at the thread I asked him for the other end of it. He gave it to me. We stood in a circle, and I carefully gave the thread to the next child encouraging him to give it to the next, and so on . . . "and now to Martin . . . and now to Petra". The whole connection hung on a thread. The rest of the children could feel that something unusual was happening. They knew Christof as a boy who never took part in anything. From then on he was co-operative, if only with small contributions. He, who had previously said: "I'm the cat" and had not tolerated hearing his name spoken, said after a few weeks "I". He put up with a game in which all the other children were animals – with this I robbed him of his special position – and tolerated my calling him Christof. In the transition period, as he was losing the cat idea, there was always something or other that he could be, that had made an impression on him. So, for instance, he said one day: 'Ich bin die Gondel" (I'm the cable car) for on Sunday he had got to the top of a mountain by this means. He was not very musical, music hardly interested him. But when one introduced a theme with technical terms such as electricity – again something without substance, he was very interested. I managed to get him to hold hands with the other children. We formed a circle and sent the current passing through our hands. We gave rhythmic impulses that were sent on; we made 'high tension' or 'low tension'. He remained with us totally active all the time.

While we watched him and his singular behaviour he gradually surrendered his autistic traits and opened out. He could then be taken into a kindergarten where he drew in the manner of

Paul Klee's line drawings of technical subjects. Now he is at school.

If music did not for the time being say anything to him – it held the group together and thus gave him an entry up the gangway. *Music* therapy must in such cases be a secondary consideration; what matters then is the social application. This is often the case. Music certainly encourages social attitudes, but if the necessary threshold of attraction for music is not reached, then it can achieve nothing. This is often the case with autistic children.

6. Suggestions for treatment

A therapy session is not fifty or thirty minutes long, but is rather a unit of time within an hour, as long as attention and concentration can be maintained. For the session to achieve anything the therapist must hold the thread in her hand and release it at the right moment.

One cannot set up any guaranteed norms, but one can give some rules so that a session flows organically and comes to a satisfactory ending. The success of a session depends upon the flexibility of the therapist.

Model sessions can be demonstrated, valuable sessions shown; it is more important, however, to know why these sessions worked. Each therapist also works so individually that for her it is her own sessions and her own plans that have validity. Each therapist should know where her strengths lie, where her secret lies and what her relationship to her material is.

Establishing contact

The therapeutic aim of the first session, whether with a group or an individual:
1. Building up trust between therapist and child through the way the right kind of contact is established.
2. Observing the visual, auditory and social reactions of the children.
3. Formulating the individual therapy plan with an optimal aim as a result of these observations.
4. Building up in the child a positive attitude to his own therapy.

1.
The first session is a very important one for it is here that weaknesses are revealed and much is already determined. It is not only important that the child comes again willingly, it is why he does so that is decisive. The first session can take a child a big step further on. He can reach a new stage, and that means: a different outlook, a different panoramic view, changes of relationship to himself and to others. The first session should change a child.

2.

The secret of observing a child closely is to make oneself empty so that one can incorporate the child within oneself. The child will express himself in some way or other, take up some kind of position, react, or he will of his own accord do something un-expected. If the therapist is willing to accept the child, she will also accept every utterance, every action the child takes. She will not reject what she deems undesirable even if it presents a paradox through lack of skill or through deliberate intention. It is something thrown out that gives insight into the child – it is diagnostically illuminating.

3

These observations lead to therapy plans. If the first session is a group session the observation is made more difficult, but the individual child will in some circumstances be stimulated to show more of himself. With the many different kinds of handicap that we treat, the forms of expression and treatment will be different. The therapist can train her memory in relation to things that happen.

4

In a group session a child can acquire a sense of distance from himself. He is no longer alone or in the centre, there are other people and things. This can be a pleasant, but also a painful experience. The fascination of the shared happening makes all the participants equal, it establishes communication, the fascination binds individuals together. Contact is not established with words or outward means.

The means of communication are carried on from the first session in a non-verbal way. Nothing is explained, the happening should be self-explanatory. It must be so constructed and so understandable that this is possible. The child comes to the session with an expecta-tion, it expects the therapists, perhaps also other children, the happening and the material. The expectation is a moment of tension. If the expectation is mixed with negative components, with anxiety, insecurity, or with the remembrance of other un-successful therapy sessions, then the first session is of particular importance. In it there must be a build-up to a positive moment of tension. The play atmosphere should lead to a state of elevation, a feeling of uplift.

Structuring the session

When the children come again they expect the familiar room, the others and the familiar material. It is the therapist's task to include something new in among these familiar elements. Repetitions are necessary and in no way minimise the excitement. The structure of the session should answer the claims of the moments of expectation in terms of the familiar and the new.

A session could be structured as follows:
1. Ritual of an acoustic-movement kind to create the atmosphere.
2. New element for therapeutic reasons.
3. Developing the situation through accepting the spontaneous creative contributions of the children. From this the following can result: a normal climax, an eccentric climax, or a non-arrival at a climax.
4. Possible corrections, working out of ideas.
5. Organic ending.

At each of the five points of the plan a friction of a positive and a negative kind can arise. It is to be reckoned with and mastered. The friction arises from the attraction, from the excitement, basically from the condition of stimulation. The boundaries within which it is to be contained will depend upon the therapist and the condition of the children. The flexibility of the plan allows for it and only with a certain tacit acceptance and a working through of these moments of friction, can a productive session arise. The therapist is not always equally in tune or prepared to give the friction enough time or to guide it successfully. The plan of the following session will be worked out on the basis of the previous one. The written notes made after the session record the important events, the individual children are written up as to their behaviour, their comments and their contributions. These observations provide a foundation for planning the next session. Sometimes it will be planned for the benefit of one child only who urgently needs help. Ideally the children should never quite leave the consciousness of the therapist – a thought here and there during the day about one or other group helps to reinforce the ties during the week.

Since the primary function of the music therapy is to take effect in a communicative, creative atmosphere, there is the danger that the happening slips out of the hand of the therapist. If this does happen once, it is not too serious, but it should not become the rule. She should have 'guiding threads' in the hand so that she can bind the group and the happening together again. A falling off of the intensity is just as undesirable as a tumult. To maintain the condition of a group session at a beneficial level of elevation, the technique of the 'guiding thread' has to be mastered.

Guiding threads★

1. Ostinato moment
2. Moment of contrast
3. Moment of surprise

These dynamic regulators can be introduced non-verbally and can take the place of the personal directive. The play sequence unfolds each time through the directional stimulus injected by the therapist. These can be adopted as long as the will and the capacity to play are there. The guiding threads are an interruption to the flow of play. As therapist one must feel exactly when this corrective is necessary and acceptable. It is possible that a momentary chaos is necessary and must be allowed to play itself out before a change is possible. One never stops learning here.

In detail: With an ostinato moment one holds the thread in the hand. It can be a verse that is sung, a spoken line of a verse, a rhythm on an instrument or also only a sound. When one plans a session, such an ostinato moment should be included. A part of the room

★   This term refers to the ball of thread that guides one through the labyrinth.

can also be designated as an ostinato place, with favourable results – a timpani in the middle to signify a gathering place and a new starting point. The words: "I'm here, you're here, we're all here together" sung to a known tune can represent an ostinato moment. In between there are individual parts that are imitated: "We do everything that Petra does". Petra's interpolated activity, with or without instrument, can show itself in three different ways: organically active; eccentrically active; inactive. The use of the ostinato moment enables the therapist to decide when to lead back from the individual activity to the neutral starting point, in this case the repetition of the words: "I'm here, you're here, etc."

The best ostinato moment within a verse that I have ever found comes from a French counting rhyme:

Toc toc toc	Toc toc toc
Il pleut sur la terre,	It rains on the earth,
toc toc toc	toc toc toc
il fait noir et clair,	it is black (dark) and light,
toc toc toc	toc toc toc
tu bats tes paupières,	you're 'batting' your eyelids,
toc toc toc	toc toc toc
tu fais des éclairs,	you're making the lightning,
toc toc toc	toc toc toc
voici le tonnerre.	here is the thunder.

The ostinato moment builds up the powers of concentration

Toc toc toc is the *ostinato moment,* the lines in between can be played out freely, the thunder at the end allows for an explosion of noise that is organically interrupted by the *toc toc toc*. The repetitions can be variously interpreted. If for the first time the verse lines were interpreted in gesture, then the second time they can be said quite functionally and rhythmically. In a third variation one can say the *toc toc toc* only internally, in a fourth variation one speaks out loud only the *toc toc toc* and the verse lines are spoken internally. With the compelling return of the ostinato moment one has everything in hand. Neither in English nor in German literature have I found a verse so ideal for this purpose.

126

With a *moment of contrast* one has a change in volume level, a change of time quality, differences of sound quality, differences between individual and group contributions. The moment of contrast helps to build flexibility but is still part of the whole through comparison. It is not usually a surprise but part of a cycle, and thereby consolidates the feeling for order.

The *moment of surprise* is initiated by the therapist, to turn away from some diversionary activity and back to the therapeutic happening. It can be a loud or a quiet signal, a visual one or a gesture. It is not prepared by the therapist like the ostinato or the moment of contrast. It grows out of the situation. There can also be a moment of surprise in a play happening, that can also be given to a child to bring about. It is expected and therefore has a high tension value.

The outsider

The outsider, described to some extent already (see p. 69) makes special demands on the therapist. He demands her patience, her flexibility, her particular inspiration. He can be an outsider through lack of challenge or because he is anxious. It is left to the inspiration of the therapist to win him over. It is especially the children or the group in which he doesn't participate and in which he achieves nothing, that compel her to develop new ideas, to make herself more sensitive to this child. Under no circumstances should she shift the blame onto him. *She* is the therapist, *she* must tune herself in, *she* must find the right wavelength. A therapist who cannot admit to herself and others – naturally not in front of the child or the group concerned – that she does not occasionally find herself confronted by a hopeless situation, excludes the possibility of further developing herself and of penetrating new areas of activity. It is often her attitude, her acquired security that is obstructing the way. In therapy one can never be quite sure, the methods, the acquired resources, should in the best cases have arisen out of situations of need. One cannot just take over a method. The need, sometimes to know nothing, belongs to the practice of therapy. The ideas that have been developed from that need are special keys that serve

127

the whole of therapy, they can become 'master keys'. A therapist who, apart from these necessary situations of need, says that therapy is exhausting is either overworked (and that she should not be) or she is not a master of her craft, or she has a false attitude. At least this is the case in paediatric music therapy. According to my experience the Orff Music Therapy has a cheering, often moving, often refreshing effect on all who come into contact with it, be they therapists, students or visitors. Though seen only once in the therapy session they say they "cannot get the children out of their heads". Names are remembered, long discussions in places far removed from the therapy room take place. The conditions are right and bearable only when the therapist also has some gain from the therapy, when she is given joy, when she is enriched.

7. Individual therapy

While in group therapy the therapist comes to the session with a plan that matches the circumstances and that should take its course in a communicative-creative atmosphere, in individual therapy one allows oneself to be stimulated by the child.

For the first session the same four points apply:

Building up confidence
Observation of the child
Formulating the individual therapy plan
Building up a positive attitude in the child

First the basis for mutual trust has to be established, meeting the child's expectation, although individual therapy is mostly conducted with children who have neither expectations nor any idea of what may be involved.

Indications

Individual music therapy is indicated for children with severe autistic traits and for those severe cases of excessive distractability, where the child is so restless that at first he can hardly stay more than ten seconds at one activity. Everything else but that which the child is doing at the moment is more interesting. The moment the activity is begun it has become uninteresting again. A child with such considerable weakness of concentration disturbs every group and must be taken individually, where through full attention being given to the one child, his concentration span can gradually be lengthened. Children with severe aggressive traits against others and against themselves should also first be given individual therapy.

Examples

A girl who had been hospitalised for four years because of a lung illness, had suffered a severe deprivation on account of this. It is difficult not to think of such a child as mentally handicapped. The speech of this six-year-old, apart from one and two-word sentences, has not developed. She had to lie a lot and now has such an unmanageable thirst for movement that one can hardly cater for it. The day passes for her in distracted restlessness. As soon as she can she has caught hold of the hair of whoever is available.

The therapist looks here for movement sequences with contrast, partly with a reciprocal giving of hands, the movement sequence being supported with words, and these, while standing still, were repeated in their sequence in clapping. Balls were carried, exchanged, reciprocally tapped. Anything acoustic on the instruments increased the restlessness and was not tolerable at all. Quiet singing and clapping, imitating rhythms calmed the child. For a short while the colours of the balls were connected with the pitches of the various chime bars (resonator bells). Her hands were always kept occupied in holding, giving, taking, picking up and so on so that they were not free to pull the therapist's hair.

The child fulfilled all challenges. Her mother was watching through the one-way screen. (To come to the session she had a long car journey to make and had to bring a second person with her to hold the child who was otherwise too restless, taking hold of her mother while she was driving, etc.) The child herself was impressed with her achievement and this helped her to improve. Praise was always interjected in the course of play. She was then able to work concentratedly for half an hour. The girl was so taken with the course of events that she did not interrupt its flow with any of her ideas. She remembered things too although there were sometimes three weeks between each session. Her stereotype echolalia disappeared, she gave instructions such as "the other way round", "once more". In the end her aggression like her restlessness was so improved that she was taken into a kindergarten, where, after an initial rebellion, she is now acceptable.

Another child, a five-year-old boy, hypersentive and distractable through brain damage, mentally handicapped, was continuously disturbing the activity. At first he only rejected everything. "No" and "you're lying" were his stereotype utterances. Access was only possible through a ball with which he played football. But he was not interested in playing a game with it; it was only the rolling ball that interested him. He took up no suggestions and it was real progress if he took the ball in his hand and threw it or rolled it. He has not yet been able to catch it. After the success with the ball he was prepared to sit for a while at the soprano xylophone and play it. Little question and answer games, one impulse receiving a counter impulse, were now possible. The large board on the wall attracted him and he 'wrote': quick scribbles, like signatures, and a conspicuous number of rectangular shapes. We came to know that his father's job involves him in technical drawing. Rhythmic movement sequences were also beneficial for this boy: walking round the large carpet carrying the jingles stick impressively, (he also could hardly bear any sound) alternating between therapist and child. This was developed into the boy walking and the therapist playing the xylophone as long as he walked, and then the therapist walking with the boy playing the xylophone in the same way.

After a few sessions he forgot the ball and the drawing on the board, but he wrote in the therapists diary – a scribble indicating his next appointment. This was important in that it showed he wanted to come again. Now his mother says he looks forward to to the sessions. The early screaming and crying have been set aside. He was one of those children who, as they come in, go straight to the prepared material, but only to clear it away, believing that the session is now at an end. Now practically all suggestions are taken up, he has a friendly basic attitude, his earlier "no" has changed to "yes". "You're lying" is no more to be heard. His attention span has lengthened considerably.

The use of music in such cases is limited to a time and rhythm challenge, that achieves a counterpart to the hypersensitive and restless distractability for a certain time. Repeated organic sequences give the child a sense of periods of time, the repetitions themselves are expected and strengthen this stabilising effect. It is particularly with the repeated and therefore familiar rhythmic sequences, underlaid throughout with texts, that the child can look at his achievement as it were, and contemplate it as an inner possession. This strengthens his understanding of the object world. So the smallest basis for sustaining an organic unit is important, because through it the time dimension can be extended. Such a beginning

131

is only fruitful when the child's attitude is positive. Sequences that are insisted upon and only mechanically executed by a crying child have no value as building material.

Another boy, Nikola, with minimal cerebral palsy and slightly spastic, threw himself with gusto onto the floor, laughed and fooled around generally throughout the session. Access to him occurred by chance for he was fascinated by a standing figure that he looked at for a long time. Three soft beaters standing on the carpet with their heads touching remained standing until with a 'tsuk' we took hold of them – he one beater and I two – they must not be allowed to fall to the ground. Two kinds of concentration were being achieved: looking at the form, inactive, then its pinpointed removal. We managed it nearly always. If we didn't he bent double with laughter and nearly fell back into his previous silly behaviour. His speech was appalling with considerable stuttering. This improved with his work in music therapy. His unstable posture was tackled with visual symmetrical sequences, first with moving beaters in the air, to the left and right, at first as in a mirror, and then each with his right and his left. He found this very funny and again nearly slipped out of control. His use of the instruments was also visually oriented: two chime bars (resonator bells) in front of him and one each to the right and left. Here strict visual and auditory imitation was demanded of him. A game using drawings delighted him and he absorbed it quietly and with concentration, he didn't laugh wildly any more and showed his joy inwardly. A card game had been prepared for the children and we took one card out of it; on it one could see the drawing of a drum, or a triangle, some jingles or a cymbal, two claves, etc. When he drew a card he took hold of the prepared instrument, named it and accompanied the therapist's recorder as rhythmically as he thought fit. If he by any chance drew the same card two or three times in succession he found that so funny that he again nearly lost balance. The therapist, however, really did want to go on playing and did not want him to get a 'wrong' card. This game with the cards can be varied in many ways. It raises the tension and brings natural moments of stillness.

After ten sessions Nikola was quieter, his speech was more distinct, and he was put into a group, where, apart from a very few exceptions, he was co-operative and almost always concentrated. If he was tired he lay down. His own achievement in the individual therapy sessions had so stabilised him that he was more secure and had more confidence. When he came to the music therapy he expected the same prepared arrangement. This was only changed in that it was extended and this stability helped his concentration. At home he had too many toys, but no person with enough regular time to play with them with him. He was subsequently accepted in a kindergarten and is now at school.

Music therapy can do much to establish a capacity for concentration: through music's inherent quality of being always on the move. The rhythmic impulses are perceived and transmitted to the sensory areas by way of the thalmic nucleus. The movement element in rhythm enables the continuous reiteration of impulses. If one can apply oneself to this rhythm in that one looks at oneself or at someone else executing it, then the quantity and quality of perception is increased; attention is aroused, and, when practised, can increase to concentration.

It is scientifically established that constant visual perception can only be maintained for a long time because the movements of the eye are continuously moving the image on the retina. In an analogy one could say that a long auditory perception is only possible through the movement of the sound itself, for instance through its rhythmic impulses. The cells in the brain, that is the nerve cells of the cortex react best to mobile stimuli. The phenomenon of music is that it is an image, an understanding or a condition only produced in movement, that can only be experienced through movement. So attention must always be present and be synchronised with what is receding and with what is approaching. The mastering of this synchronising demands concentration, its practice, however, can also develop concentration. A repeated rhythm, a repeated melodic interval in pitch, a *pattern* in fact, helps concentration, for small repeated units are attractive. The following of new impulses that are additional to this ground pattern creates a second stage of attention. A sustained unit of sound in which the rhythmic impulses are not made evident is less helpful to concentration.

The following description will show how a therapy session can sometimes go off the rails and yet be therapeutically effective:

I can remember the first session with a five-year-old boy, U., who was generally retarded in development. The person who accompanied him, since it was to be a music therapy session, had brought a drum. So far so good. But she banged it incessantly and penetratingly and wanted to interest U. with it. He just held his hands over his ears all the time. He will have to get used to it, thought the adult – rather wide of the mark.

The child withdrew into a corner, lay on the ground and turned a soft beater round and round in his hand. Now the therapist was supposed to intervene. "He'll pull that beater quite to pieces if we don't take it away from him". Why shouldn't he pull it to pieces? At that moment it was the only thing that interested him. I touched his beater with mine, and as if by chance I touched him too. He accepted this. An encounter. He was already prepared for the next. In the following minutes we had an intensive beater game, full of wit and understanding, meeting and avoiding one another, and exchanging beaters – it was quite quiet between us, no drum disturbed us, a relationship had been established through material. By chance our eyes met, and we both found it pleasant. I have never 'brought about eye contact', a main insistence of psychologists, who can often only manage it after weeks of painstaking effort. In most cases it happens in the first session. The sensitive therapist will accept it almost shyly, it is after all a gift and the first sign of relationship.

We had two kinds of contact, through the beaters, that by now were playing a virtuoso game togther, and now and then through eye-contact. Through the beaters we developed rhythm and transparent play. It happened that I felt the child's hand and it was rough. I thought it might be a good idea to put some hand cream on it. Cream was brought and I carefully rubbed it in, first onto the one hand and then the other. My hand also profited from the same cream and the same process. Here was another relationship that the child accepted – skin contact of a very intensive kind. All this happened without an exchange of words between us. The drum lay on the floor. What happened? U. went to the drum, sat down, picked it up and played it. He carried his experience of touching over to the drum. Without having been shown he played the drum with quiet regular beats. From then on he was away. Contact had been entered into. Making use of the situation that arises is so often the surest stimulus for the child.

In her way too a twelve-year-old girl knew how to make use of a situation. She usually came with a younger boy with a quite different character. They would not yield to one another in their fantasy play. At first the boy predominated: dangerous things came into the conversation, fire, ghosts, the themes were played out. Drawing fire and washing the board afterwards with water helped these anxieties. He could draw an apartment block with perhaps fourteen floors, tall and narrow, with only two windows at the front. "It's burning there at the top and the door's got stuck" – the fire engines came mostly too late. These representations were not to be denied, they would come suddenly after musical contributions. The boy had a strong personal rhythm; weddings and wedding music was also a favourite theme with him. The playing out of his anxieties did help him and the girl assisted mostly as ambulance nurse. It happened that she sometimes came alone to the session and she made immediate use of this situation. She told her own stories starting with babyhood. The story was carried by her singing voice stimulated by the small soprano metallophone. The objects lying around her were given representative functions. A triangle was the cradle, its beater the baby. The individual beaters were doctor, hired girl, grandmother, father. She took the role of mother herself. If the therapist made a mistake with the beaters she was immediately rebuked and corrected: "The blue beater is the father" (no significance in the colours). Names were chosen, the baby getting the best one, one that was similar to the child's own. The mother was very busy and often had guests. The doctor often called, things happened, time passed. The baby would grow several months in one session but was never older than eleven months, it remained a baby. The girl managed the synchronisation of time remarkably though at school she had no understanding for mathematics. She managed her household superbly, sent the maid for orders, arranged for guests in the evening, other visitors arrived, they drove into the country, she had to telephone. When asked for the number she gave the area code and her own number. She told the whole story in song and accompanied herself. She thereby managed her emotions and

135

presented an objective attitude to herself in the often moving descriptions. Later the absent boy was the father, who died, and she arranged the funeral ceremony and also decided on the music. Later on the absent boy became a grown-up son. The music therapy had become a play therapy without prepared objects like dolls, kitchen materials etc. In later representations she needed actual objects no more, but carried an imaginary baby herself, and her concern for it was remarkable, everything had to be very quiet.

In discussion with the psychologists it was possible to effect a change of school. The girl is more capable than she mostly shows. In general she is more attentive and can concentrate better at school. Her restless nature has also improved. She lives for her therapy sessions and misses them when they are not given. The baby phase is no longer played out; music is now entirely in the foreground. We are trying to bring to life her understanding for mathematics.

8. The relationship between parents and therapists

When parents bring their children to music therapy they come with an expectation. They have meanwhile been through the out-patients department, a case history has been built up, and a picture of the illness has been traced back into the past, to the birth and the pregnancy, in order to find some clues. The diagnosis, based on this picture and various examinations and tests, stipulates a therapy according to the nature of the case.

Music therapy is indicated in those cases where there are problems of contact and where the social development is disturbed – the child is shy or too direct and aggressive – where there are problems of co-ordination that show themselves in clumsiness, and at school age in reading difficulties for instance, where there are speech and hearing handicaps and where there is an all round retardation of development. There is hardly a case for which music therapy should not be indicated and where the Orff Music Therapy cannot make some inroads and effect some improvement.

According to the kind of case, the child is either placed in a group or given individual therapy. In a group session four, five or six children assemble near the therapy room, they have taken off their outdoor clothing and, relinquished by their father or mother for a while they will experience a therapy session together. The children are given therapy without their parents for the following reasons:

The children should form a relationship with each other as a group,
The children should not feel that they are being watched.

If a mother takes part in a group session she will watch first and foremost her own child. She will discover that her child reacts faster, slower, more skilfully, less skilfully than the other children. In the rarest of cases she will notice this for herself and keep it to herself. She is more likely to say to the child (her observations may be correct): "Why didn't you ... didn't you notice ... " or at home she will make comments to the family and the child will hear them. The child receives a mirrored image of his achievement, a value judgement, and here even positive comments are just as damaging. For the therapist it is not important for the child to show himself at his best – she is always hearing the same final instructions from parents to their children: "do your best, be a good boy, pay attention now" – what she wants is for the child to show his real self, that he shows just something of what he is, thinks, would like to be, doesn't have, doesn't want to do, etc. The therapist registers this, makes a note of it and will try to lead the child in the light of what he reveals of himself.

When their mother is present the children have one eye on her: "What will she think, is that right?" The motives for this can often be of a positive nature, but the child still has his attention divided between his mother and the group. The mother is an outsider, though it is a different case when she joins in and this is possible in individual cases, though this can make other unstable children jealous. The child in this case must not come between the therapist and the other children. The therapist is there for all of them, participating with them, uniting them, but also preserving detachment.

The session should, and mostly does, result in a special experience, and the child leaves with this experience. Outside the door he finds the familiar world again. This should not rob the child of the unusual circumstances he has just lived through. Words such as: "Were you a good boy, did you do as you were told, get dressed quickly, shake hands, say thank-you" will fall upon a child suddenly and interrupt abruptly his state of mind. A mother should see that her child's eyes are alive, shining, that he wants to steep his eyes in those of his mother, to let her take part in quiet understanding "that it was great". Often the children throw themselves into their mother's arms, the most fitting end. The child doesn't want to say: "I was very good, I was the best, the first, the only one, I didn't understand, I couldn't follow". Perhaps on the homeward journey, unasked, he will volunteer something, or first say something when he is at home, perhaps to his teddy bear or doll. The child – I can say this after receiving many kinds of corroboration – looks forward to the next meeting, for many children it is the best moment of the week. Or he may be a little anxious about the next session for some internal reason: perhaps he found the bass drum too loud, or he regrets that he did not play the triangle, or that he is not so good at skipping. He will come again, though, and one can then make good his misgivings.

In the therapy and particularly in the group therapy, the children experience something of their world, and to some extent, its secret. It should be enough for the parents that their child comes joyfully to them and that he looks forward to the next session with excitement.

If there is an opportunity the therapist will speak to the parents. Under no circumstances should she do so in front of the child. Parents' words such as: but my child is so slow, wild, uncontrolled or whatever, stamp the child with the word in a corresponding way. The child has heard it so often from an environment that leaves its mark on him. He conforms to this qualitative judgement. Therefore it is good when a child can show a different side of himself, something new, and throw off the gradual accretion of behaviour attributed to him. It is not always so, but often. After a session I gladly say to all mothers together: "It was a good session and they all took part very well," without any individual judgement. If there is an opportunity to talk about one child one should give a true comment on the child's behaviour and his contribution, and let the mother tell what she wants to tell, and from this one gets a more complete picture of the child.

In exceptional cases the mother can be present, because the child is so shy that he will never come into the first session alone. The mother will then watch at a certain distance, or they both sit apart together, or they both join in. It is difficult with very small adopted children. It is understandable that they are anxious – one has to judge each case as it comes.

There are therapies where father or mother become co-therapists, where the children can and should practise at home. It seems to me that music therapy does not come into this category.

In the group situation the child has experiences, lives through situations that cannot be brought about at home. The child offers his own contribution, because he is stimulated through the sound that they all produce, through the play situation that arises out of the various social relationships, and he goes home imbued with the whole complex, and not with rhythms or intervals that he has learnt. If, however, the child wants to do something at home that was done in the session and he needs a partner, then his father or mother should be prepared to give time for this and allow the child to lead them. Perhaps he also wants to include his siblings in this play situation, that he has stored in his memory. One should at the very least have the time to listen. The participation that the child felt in the group session can be reproduced through such a co-operation, and the child will also be practising. It is not only a question of reproducing some kind of rhythm accurately, but of how that rhythm and ones relationship to it fit into the whole happening.

Once a child has mastered something one does not insist on a repetition if he is not prepared for it. A child should be able to use something he has mastered as he likes. In this context, during the car drive to the therapy session, a child had sung something that had been part of the previous session. She was one of a group of mongoloid children whose parents had got their way and were sitting in on the sessions. During the session each child had the opportunity to sing this song. When it was B.'s turn she wanted to start, looked at her mother, hesitated and nothing came. Without giving her time her mother burst in upon the situation with the words: "You were singing it all the way here in the car, sing it why don't you, you know it." Her mother was abashed that her child was not accomplishing anything in front of the other children and particularly in front of the other mothers. Perhaps if the child had not felt the pressure to achieve from her mother she would have accomplished her contribution at the right time. I can imagine how on the return journey the reproaches "why didn't you sing it" were continued.

But there are also positive situations with mothers, and then usually when they sit in the circle and join in. The attitude of critical surveyal arises through the distance and this is no longer there when they participate. The mothers also come into a relationship with one another. When children have quadriplegia and are quadrispastic and cannot even sit without assistance, then the parents are a help as co-therapists as it were. They try at home with similar kinds of animation to stimulate the necessary movements. It also means a lot to these mothers of children with these severe handicaps, to be able to talk to one another about identical or similar cases and they often exchange practical experiences with one another.

The one-way screen provides one further way for a mother to participate. From the room next door it is transparent, from the therapy room it looks like a mirror. The child is alone with the therapist, the parents watch. Afterwards one can discuss the activity and the behaviour of the child. Video tape films can also be made from such an observation room. One can also turn the situation round and the therapist can watch the behaviour of parent and child through the one-way screen. The feeling of being watched soon goes once one is in the therapy room.

A close contact between therapist and mother is needed. The child mirrors himself differently in each of them. It is always his face, one in the familiar situation, the other in the unusual one. One must have patience and allow the child to bring these two situations together. Therapist and mother should avoid thinking of the face that they see as *the* face. A child who is too seldom challenged and rather protected at home will find the therapy session relatively demanding; he has to establish a balance. A child who is much corrected at home, where his bad or his good aspects are being continually remarked upon, will find himself in an unusual situation in the music therapy session with its mostly non-directive approach and its non-verbal atmosphere; he too has to establish a balance. It is up to the balancing powers of the child to work through the impulses and situations of a therapy session within his home atmosphere. If he is supported in this at home, and if the support is more in the nature of a temporising attitude rather than a repetitious and demanding attitude, then there will be no inner conflict. The therapy is then at its most effective and enduring. The children are given bodily nourishment by their parents. The assimilation and processing of this nourishment takes place *inside* the child without any contribution from them. In therapy the children are supplied with a nourishment necessary to them, and it is only within the child that the processing of these benefits takes place.

141

9. Some case histories

L. is a ten-year-old boy, who after meningitis when he was three is now diagnosed as suffering from partial deafness of the inner ear. His mother is deaf in one ear and nearly blind. His medical notes say: Disturbance of speech development after meningitis, since then hard of hearing and a regression of speech development. The boy understands no questions, carries out no tasks given to him in speech, occasionally understands when instructions are supported by gestures and are connected with people. He doesn't notice noises and musical sounds, nor clapping; a sound played to him is not copied. A supplementary diagnosis presumes aphasia with lack of understanding for speech and recommends that the child should under no circumstances be sent back to an institute for the deaf and dumb. The aetiology is not clear, i.e. the causes for disturbed hearing and the resultant behaviour are not established.

The observations of L.'s case are from ten years ago, but thanks to detailed notes they can be reconstructed. In addition the important occurrences have remained vividly in the memory.

L. was in a group of eight children with an average age of ten and with various handicaps. The children were in a residential home and went to school there. L. was included in the group as a child with hearing and speech defects. He wore a hearing aid and was treated by me in the same way as the other children. In my notes I wrote after the first session: "L. walks clapping out of the session, and continues outside, lost in thought."

L. was now exposed to whatever happened in the group. To spoken texts clapping was added, the instruments were explored, the technique of playing them was discovered through considering their acoustical characteristics: the long reverberation of the metallophone, for instance, needed fewer sounds than the short sound of a xylophone. On the barred instruments melodies were invented and copied, first using the pentatonic scale based on C, on F and on G. The individual melodies were accompanied by drone bass type ostinati. In lively sessions in which each child was allowed to interrupt with ideas and suggestions, the children became a small community at play. The concentration and the tolerance of one another increased, so that the purely musical accomplishment

142

became more 'hearable'. The children were free and felt free; they were prepared to accept a basic rhythm as obligatory, and in the same way the limitation to a particular scale. This gave them the freedom to express themselves. Lively rhythmic structures arose of their own accord:

Plant the seed well,
care for the tree,
for who can tell
how tall it will be?

There are birds in a tree – there were many offers to play and whistle various bird sounds, the woodpecker on the hollow edge of the xylophone box, etc.

L. took part in everything, he was not particularly helped, he looked to it and did what he could. This boy, who was at first quite withdrawn with a neutral facial expression, became almost mischievous with an alert expression and full participation in everything that was happening. The group was having its effect.

Through his mother's handicap L. had had to do without encouraging words, verses and rhymes. He soaked up the acoustical atmosphere in our sessions. His capacity for inner hearing was conspicuous. When he played a melody and by mistake played on a different bar from the one intended, he winced visibly at this irritation. During these sessions, through constant practice, he acquired a knowledge of the different interval relationships and then played melodies without mistakes.

His social attentiveness increased. At a rehearsal for a Christmas play in which he was playing himself, he listened and looked attentively at the others. In subsequent rehearsals it was discovered that from behind the curtain, where he could see nothing, he was swaying in time to the music. The child had thus revealed more about the state of his hearing than any test situation could. In echo games – the therapist plays first, the children copy (and also the other way round) – L. was allowed to use his eyes as well as his ears and the visual element had certainly been a help to him. His horror at a wrong note showed, however, how much he was using his ears. After the third session he left off his hearing aid.

So far L. had met all challenges and had taken up suggestions; he had copied, he had invented. In the tenth session he surprised us with a spontaneous counterpoint to the melody "Spiel mir auf".

He had felt the rhythm and the melody so strongly that he had the confidence to play it.

L., who for a long time had been in an institute for the deaf and dumb and who also had no one talking to him at home, had become quite mute as the years went by. That he heard and listened was ever more obvious as the description of the following game will prove: We were playing with the strokes of a bell – the individual children wanted to be woken and we gave L. the task of striking the bell. 'At six o'clock' – he played six chords, 'at nine o'clock' – nine chords. He always got it right.

The breakthrough to speech within the time we were together came about as follows:
We used this text

Wolf, Wolf friss mi nit!	Wolf, Wolf, don't eat me
Hundert Taler gib i dir nit,	I'll not give you a hundred Taler,★
zehn will ich dir geben,	Ten Taler will I give
lass mich nur am Leben.	If you'll only let me live.

The text was sung to a striking melody, supported by a powerful ostinato. The wolf was played in person. Baring his teeth he ran round in a circle striking fear into the hearts of his supposed victims. The boy chosen for this role – severe behaviour disturbance and aggression, his behaviour improved gradually – played the part so

★ Pounds or dollars could be substituted here.

144

that one really was afraid. He came to a stand before mute L. and said: "You have to pay me". The rules were that the ten had to be counted out rhythmically in some way or other such as:

1,2,3, – 4,5,6, – 7,8,9, – 10!
1,2,3,4,5, – 6,7,8,9,10!
1 – 2/3,4,5, – 6 – 7/8,9,10!

And now the unbelievable happened: L. counted from one to nine in one rush – 123456789 – here he stopped and pretended to look for his tenth Taler, where was it? Not in the right pocket . . . nor the left . . . not in the trouser pocket . . . not in the back pocket . . . no, where? There, at the last moment he found it in the little breast pocket and handed it over mischievously with the word "ten"! The game went on. The children had noticed the sensation, however, and as we played back the tape on which we had been recording it they said: "L. . . . you spoke, do speak again!" but he remained silent. The game was played further to its end, the wolf was tired and laid himself down and snored – loudly and energetically. The children came close to him, stole the money from him and laughed at him. There again L.'s monotone voice was heard saying: "Der Wolf soll sagen, zum Kuckuck, wo ist mein Geld!" (The wolf should say, darn it, where is my money). He had been so carried away by the game that he overcame his muteness and spoke.

Result

The music therapy sessions directed the boy towards auditory experience. He wanted to take part. His hearing disability was outweighed by his interest and his innate musicality helped him to achieve this. His playing with melodic shapes, his extension and reduction of these showed that he was musical. The marked clumsiness of his left hand mentioned in his case notes was not noticeable. The contact with the group, at first hesitant, became friendly. His general physical skill increased, he was finally able to dive through a forward rolling hoop and land on a mat.

The music therapy was able to clarify the diagnosis. The musical activity gave the boy self-affirmation and social experience. Some years later he became an apprentice and got on well.

145

A.K.

Diagnosis

Mentally handicapped, speech and general development retarded, disturbed behavour.

From the notes

1. We would rather have removed him from the group. Almost incessantly he groaned out his displeasure loudly and ostentatiously and held his hands over his ears. He touched no one and tolerated no contact from others, he was unbearable. He was always looking towards the door and wanting to go out.

2. In the second session he is prepared to sit with us on the floor but he still touches nothing. He still croaks and groans.

3. In the third session he is prepared to play but only when I hold his beater with him. He is passive and limp.

4. In the game "The drum goes round, don't you look round' – one child walks round the circle with the drum, finally stops by someone and says: "You look round", this chosen one now walks round with the drum. Today A. is chosen twice. Getting up from the floor is difficult for him, he allows me to help him and is then prepared to walk round with me. He smiles a little. Occasionally he still holds his hands over his ears, his groaning is better.

5. Today in the song "Es tanzt ein Bibabutzemann"* A. goes into the middle and "rüttelt sich und schüttelt sich" (he jiggled round and joggled round). This he does not actually do but stands in the middle as long as we sing the song, then turns towards me and gives me a fond look.

6. Playing with the drum, free choice on how to handle it. A. has his own inspiration: he puts it on his head.

7. Today A. played with help in the verse: One, two three, the hen's laid an egg for me, a white egg she's laid for me, one, two, three. We have three wood blocks and decide in which one the hen has laid her egg; that is the one that is played.

8. Each one accompanies a recorder melody with the gestures of their choice. Today A. is very fierce.

9. After a long gap A. comes today, happy and pleased to be here

* Orff-Schulwerk, *Lieder für die Schule*, II, No. 8, publ. Schott, Mainz.

146

again. No groaning, no hands over the ears. He participates, also in walking. Each plays his own name in a individual way on the drum, one child with fingertips, one with his fist, and A. with his knee!

10. We walk in 'snake' formation, one behind the other, one leads. At a signal the whole snake lies down "Rast und Ruh"... (rest and quiet). Since A cannot squat he lies down completely, although this is very difficult for him and needs courage.

11. A. joins in everything happily. We play "Night". At the sound of the big cymbal it is night. Animals come. A. joins in and makes some vocal sounds.

12. The verse:

Wiss ihr was,	D'you know what
wenns regnet, wirds nass,	when it rains, it's wet,
wenns schneit, wirds weiss,	when it snows, it's white,
wenns brennt, wirds heiss,	when it burns, it's hot,

is played out. One has to guess if it is raining or snowing, storm and wind are introduced as well. The mentally handicapped group has become active. A. plays with big sounds on the drum, he holds it quite naturally now, he tackles all challenges and has good eye contact. Sometimes he speaks a word or two, awkwardly. He listens too when others are playing. A. now lies quite quietly when we are playing "Night", and lies down and sleeps, to be woken again with the little cymbals.

13. Today A. walks with the drum held high. He plays it powerfully with a beater. Not a weak child any more, he plays it almost defiantly, quite alone and retains the beater in his hand. When he plays the last beat, that for us means 'halt' everyone has to remain standing. With A. there are many last beats today; he enjoys the fact that the others have to stop and stand.

14. Today another boy wanted to take hold of A. He didn't like it and fell back into his groaning.

15. Joins in everything well, plays bass xylophone energetically, but I am the only one who may touch him.

16. Today A. was good in a contrast game: he gave one beat, the therapist the next, in successful opposition. Now we must brake his forte playing, he switches then to an agreeable piano.

17. A. now gives rhythms that I imitate, since I get them right he laughs because he is pleased.

18. A. loves the drum, but he flatly refuses the little jingles. He accompanies my recorder playing well and correctly on the drum, the other children walk, skip, jump.

Result

A. has achieved contact with the therapist and thereby with the group. To the end he was still reluctant to give his hand to another child or to clap another's hand. He only allowed me to touch him. He has developed a good relationship to objects, though, and handles them firmly. He participated in what was happening and behaved reliably. He still has antipathies to certain objects, but he has put aside his aggressive, provoking behaviour that was coupled with passivity.

Corinna had fallen off her horse and had suffered a brain contusion that had caused severe brain damage. She used only stereotype patterns of speech and according to her diagnosis she had a sensory aphasic speech disturbance. She was seventeen years old.

This attractive girl, Corinna, came one day into a group of adolescent girls who were difficult to educate. She had fallen from her horse when out riding and had brain damage and had lost her memory, they said. She did not know where she was going, where she came from, what yesterday was nor what she had done in the past. As I offered her something to do she said: "Yes, I don't know," "Yes, I can't."

We played a question–answer game on the instruments: a girl walks round past the prepared xylophones and metallophones, etc., a beater in her hand. She stops by one of the instruments and plays a few sounds. One can make the question slow or fast, one can answer short or long. An exciting and witty situation develops. As Jutta stands before Corinna, Corinna says: "Yes, I can't", "Yes, I don't know." I interpolate: "No one knows what Jutta is going to ask, only the here and now counts and that is what you answer". I ask: "Are you here now?" "Yes, of course", she answers and she does it nicely. Now she has to go and ask someone else. "I can't". I interpolate: "You could ask, shall we go out on the Meadows?"

(the Munich Oktoberfest was just in full swing). Her answer: "But that's a silly question, we won't go at all; and if we go we'll go with my father." It was not a game situation to her but reality, but at least it had broken her stereotype way of speaking. To this I said: "You're right" and asked her a proper question: "Do you like to come here, have you enjoyed it?" She answered: "Yes, of course, I've enjoyed it."

In the next sessions she repeated her stereotype "I don't know". Nevertheless when she played some notes on my instrument and I copied them exactly she said: "Yes, that's right."

In one of the next sessions we played the song *Kein schöner Land in dieser Zeit**. She managed to play the melody. She joins in everything and seems glad. After the session she said: "But where do I go now, I don't know." I take her to her room. In a further session she says spontaneously: "I know how the scale goes: c, d, e, f, g, a, b, c."

A while later she was sitting again behind her metallophone, it was her favourite, and while the rest of us were busy with the question and answer game she was trying something out. Suddenly the other girls were nudging one another and pointing. What was the matter? Corinna started to play and managed *Kein schöner Land* faultlessly. We then played it with her. She had remembered that we had played it some weeks previously and also how to play it on the instrument.

She had now quite lost the earlier "I don't know, I can't". She was interested in playing and she remembered melodies. In conversations she answered correctly when the question was sensible. If she were not addressed as befitted her age she did not react. I once said to her: "The boys' group is not for you, they are too rough". To which she said spontaneously: "Why not, I have a brother." When asked: "How old is your brother?" she answered: "He was born in 1957." She now counted: "57,58,59,60,61,62,63, 64,65 – then he's eight years old, that's right." (and it was, I checked). When it came to languages she showed some improbable memories and striking reactions. Quite by chance I once said in English: "Now it's finished." She answered spontaneously in English "Yes"!

* A German folk song.

I spoke further in English and she answered in English. I asked her if she knew French. "I start French first in the sixth grade (which was quite right) but I know Latin." I said: "hortus, hortus bellus," and I meant, how strange that hortus should be masculine. She immediately said in German: "In German, garden is also masculine". I carry on: "bellissima would be nice", to which she says: "then lets say horta bellissima." I say further both *pater* and *mater* and she translates these into *English* – father, mother! I then ask her how long she will stay here, and she says: "I don't know".

I know nothing about the further development of this girl. I only know that in her other working sessions she immediately digressed, gave no more answers and sat staring in front of her. The music sessions had kept her always awake. The sessions were interrupted by a year's commitment in America. Someone wrote to me that after six months Corinna had said: "I want to stay here until Frau Orff comes back."

Detlef has retarded development after an infectious illness with complications. At two and a half years he cannot yet walk without help, does not speak and hardly understands speech. Severe autistic behaviour hinders any access to him.

Hand in hand with the psychologist a boy with a small, heavy body and a very large head moved slowly towards my room. Would I be able to do anything with him, I thought. I placed him against the wall so that he could sit more securely. He immediately started to knock on the wall with the back of his hand in a stereotype way. We did not exist for him at all. He was there and there was a wall that he was not feeling and touching but that he was experiencing as a boundary. The same movement was now continued on the carpet. Here I made my attack: I made a clear beat on the carpet, but with the palm of my hand. The child did the same. The whole situation had turned round 180 degrees. It was a real turnabout. Here was a stimulus situation to which the child responded. A drum was pushed towards him. He played on it in his way with the back of his hand. I stimulated him by playing on it with the palm side of my hand. He imitated again. We had established our contact. He digressed again and knocked on the wall in the old way, came back to the drum, however. He allowed me to guide his hand to the sung words:

Det-lef plays,   Det-lef, Det-lef,   Det-lef plays

In this way he accompanied on the drum. He smiled. More had happened than I expected. The psychologist thought it was the best that he had so far achieved.

From this the following therapy plan was drawn up:

1. To extend awareness of the environment
For him the world is an arch with a radius of perhaps two metres and an angle left and right of 45 degrees at the most. Nothing that happened outside that arch was perceived.

2. To build on and extend his willingness to imitate
Now and then he reacts to a stimulus of a gesticular-acoustical nature. These should become more reliable and stop him from digressing and withdrawing to his inner world.

3. To build up an understanding for dialogue
Reliable imitation will build up an understanding for dialogue, though it is not important that the imitation is always 'right', as long as it occupies the same amount of time.

In the second session a drum and two beaters were prepared. He was seated on the carpet. He recognised the drum and made contact with it. He played it with the back and front of his hand. As the recorder played a melody he drummed spontaneously to it. He tolerated having his hand clapped with that of the therapist and thus touching her. Then he took the two beaters that were lying there and made them almost do a kind of dance on the drum, for he was holding them at the extreme end and handled them like marionettes. He then changed to using them for playing the drum and changed immediately from holding them with the fingers to holding them with his hands. He listened then to the recorder playing and gave the therapist a profound look with his large,

151

blue eyes. His look could change from a veiled, passive one to a pulsating one. He smiled a little and made some la, la and humming sounds.

In the third session a considerable extension of environmental awareness came about. Two drums were played, he turned to the chime bars (resonator bells) that were being played to his right and left, he looked up to the large cymbal as he heard it sound over his head. He was lifted up and immediately touched the cymbal as it vibrated over his head. Later he touched it with his beaters. But when it was held further away from him he no longer followed it with his eyes.

In the fourth session he immediately took the beaters and played the drum coming from quiet into loud playing – a crescendo. That pleased him. He turned to the board – a green one going down to floor level on which one can draw – and played on it with his beaters. Two quickly-drawn circles representing two drums were played accurately with good aim. Then he played the big cymbal again and this impressed him very much – he looked up to it again and touched it. A new thing that he did was to play a chime bar that lay in front of him while the cymbal was still sounding. He bent himself right forward to reach the chime bar, and reached out to one that lay behind him.

In the fifth and sixth sessions he handled everything that was round him, bent over towards things and played them with initiative. The therapist therefore took over the role of the imitator. As Detlef once consciously played a minor third and listened for her reply, she played the same third on the recorder, and he looked up to her with an understanding look as if to say: "You did that well!" Sometimes he responded to challenges, by chance? His mother confirmed that he did occasionally do so at home.

The treatment for the time being was at an end. Music therapy had been effective as the only therapy. As a result the child was able to walk without help at home.

When he came again after four months he was able to run round the room alone and he made good use of this. Many different kinds of instrument stood at his disposal. In contrast to self-chosen stereotypes that satisfied for a long time, this autistic child became involved in challenges that were strange to him for only a short time. So he found the bass drum, bass xylophone, small and large cymbal, a bongo drum, small articles of one kind or another and finally a hoop. This revealed the great strides that he had made in that he regarded these things, took them up or rejected them, and that his environment awareness had increased to maximum capacity through his independent walking. He was interested in the whole room, he went to the cupboards and even unlocked them. He made vocal sounds occasionally and one-word sentences, but still very hesitantly.

Undernourished and neglected, Renée was hospitalised soon after birth. About the birth and the family case history there was no further information. Renée came to our Kinderzentrum (children's centre) at three and a half years old and first learnt to sit here. She was a case of severe deprivation with considerable psychomotor retardation and with additional early brain damage. She had stereotype behaviour, no eye contact, no speech and no understanding of speech and she resisted contact. She was so tense that one could assume that she was quadrispastic, and so it was stated in her diagnosis.

A thin little girl with a bird face sat opposite me. She struck her chin in a stereotype way at frequent intervals while looking absently upwards. As I played a chime bar (resonator bell), she looked, took a beater herself and turned it quickly in her hand. As I stimulated her by striking her beater with mine she intensified her twiddling. In the course of the session our first contact came through the beaters in that we took it in turns to strike one another's beaters. Renée twitched at this but this provocation still had a positive effect, she became more awake, almost jolly. She played a drum that stood nearby and there then arose alternating beats in quite long, even sequences: one beat from her, one from me. It is impossible for her to play something that stands *in front of* her, she is too tense, but to the right and left works well. Her symmetrical treatment of the situation is noticeable.

In the second session we again have symmetrical beats, left and right on drums, alternating with stereotype behaviour. Suddenly she collapses into herself. Hearing unexpected sounds she twitches and draws herself together, but one has the feeling that this is a helpful provocation. A second, intentionally provoking sound finds her prepared. Sometimes *she* provokingly knocks my two beaters apart with her own and her aim is good. She allows herself to be stimulated and then takes over the initiative.

In the next session I try to get her to play with her beaters directly in front of her. A small metallophone is placed lengthways in front of her, she doesn't touch it, nor a glockenspiel placed similarly. She falls back into her stereotype chin-beating for which the beater comes in handy. Carefully this is interrupted. To relax her tension I take her hands, and she takes each of my forefingers in her hands. Joined together in this way I try to come to a circular movement while singing with obviously appropriate words, and shake her to the left and right; she becomes looser, she smiles. I try to cross her hands, impossible, she puts up every possible resistance. After trying for a long time she becomes less resistant and finally it is achieved – a breakthrough.

In the next session a pair of bongo drums are so placed that we each have one of the two drums in front of us. It works: Renée plays her drum, that is she plays *in front of* her, she has her hands near one another, she is relaxed. She goes beyond the challenge when she plays my drum with her beater, she has to stretch out her hand forwards to do so. Here she granted me her first profound look; her bird-like face became very human. A little later she speeded up her even beats on her drum, the sound increased.

The next session is portrayed in photographs (F and G). We see the bird-like Renée and the human being, addressed and surrendering. This is a new facial expression, it has developed in the eight sessions of intensive work.

Because of other commitments and Renée being ill there is a gap of nearly three months. Now when she plays with the beaters, she throws them behind her after a little while. Since this is repeated we stop this activity for the time being. We try to extend her narrow range of vision. A drum is held to the left, then to the right, she follows it every time with her eyes. She can stand now but does so most unwillingly and tenses up very much. Nevertheless she is placed by the bass drum and tolerates having it played. She holds on tight and feels the vibrations. But she will only play it when she is sitting. The big bass drum stick is a new challenge. She retains it in her hand for the next twenty-five minutes and often plays the bass drum with it, visibly an event for her. She uses the following technique: many quick beats on the big drum skin, then she swings the beater away and enjoys the resonance. She waits till the skin has stopped vibrating before she gives new impulses. To prevent this from becoming stereotype two coloured circles are painted on the drum. Very precisely she plays in either the larger or the smaller circle. After this intensive play experience she sits quietly, the beater still in her hand and starts babbling, sounds or intervals that cannot be distinguished.

In the following sessions small beaters are again thrown away after a short time and she picks up new ones. She claps, sometimes rhythmically, to a recorder melody and is then prepared to imitate hand gestures and to come into a dialogue relationship. Today she sings a falling minor third accurately and plays it rhythmically with her beaters on the floor. This she did spontaneously.

Today she plays specific rhythms on the bass drum for a long time:

She is quite alert, with little stereotype behaviour, she stands for a long time by the bass drum and listens to the recorder.

Another gap of eight weeks, but from now on continuous music therapy over three months with considerable results. She shows visible pleasure as she is fetched again. Since she is still throwing the beaters down a hoop is set between us as a link. It is lifted high, turned, shaken, she enjoys this and keeps her hands on it.

On the next day she remembers this and it is *she* who starts to lift it high. She contributes a new variation, she swings it to left and right and this gives back a sound from the carpeted floor. After a while she tries doing this with only one hand, with the left, with the right, the therapist helping each time. Then she bends forward and strikes the floor and then the carpet, quite intentionally and two different sounds result. Then she takes two beaters and plays the bongos, puts the beaters aside and comes back to the hoop. Here she speaks a word that is not understood. She takes a beater and tries to lift the hoop with it, then she knocks the hoop down again. Two therapists sit beside her. After the session she stands relaxed, shows her pleasure and is then led to the door, though her arms are still very tense.

10th October: She now has a session nearly every day and she deserves it. As soon as she is sitting she spontaneously goes through all the activities with the hoop that she experienced in the last two sessions. She reacts immediately to the word "Halt", she makes several verbal utterances, she smiles, she is alert. Stereotype behaviour is not seen any more. She points quite definitely to the larger recorder, lying prepared with the others, and guides it into my mouth. After listening attentively, she accompanies with both hands on the bongos.

11th October: She handles the hoop superbly. Then she accompanies the recorder with the bongos. At the end she beats rapidly with both hands making a drum roll, the recorder answers with a trill, a high one and a low one. This pleases her. She asks for the high one, quite definitely the high one – if the low one comes she reachers out for the recorder and practically rams it into the therapist's mouth. When the high one comes she is satisfied and reacts with quick beats on the bongos. She makes an important sound contribution when she sings the minor third with the upper whole tone:

She is led out, she is relaxed and is singing. She looks consciously at the guests who are present.

15th October: Today she points to the smaller, white recorder, she wants to hear that one. She accompanies on the bongos, as she hears the final trill she reacts with a roll on her drums.

Today the following were heard and written down:

She no longer throws the beaters down.

156

16th October: Today this was
written down

To this major third we heard a drawn out word like 'nimm'. It was part of a longer sequence spoken in this rhythm:

In spite of the repeated rhythm this was not reckoned to be a stereotype for the volume of sound increased and decreased.

Then as if sung:

i ma – ma i ma – ma   then   je – a, je – a,

then sung:

ni ni – ni ni na   la – la la

then abbreviated
in a rhythm in threes

ni – ni – na   ni – ni – na

then like an upward
octave leap

then the reverse from high to low

ia – – – – – – – – – –

17th October: As she was fetched she articulated her pleasure in vocal sounds.

a a a a a spoken on one note

She played on the bongos with one beater

and afterwards laid the beaters down, she did not throw them. This now happens repeatedly.

She reacted to the even pulse of the therapist as follows:

She changed her beater from the right to the left hand, she took hold of the therapist's beater.

She played with the therapist, at first purposely one after the other and then simultaneously

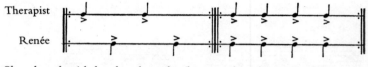

She played with her hand on the drum and spoke as she did so

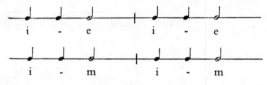

One hears anja anja eieiei

With this last slow singing she lies relaxed with the hoop on the floor.

23rd October: She plays the same rhythm for some time

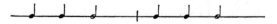

The therapist supports this rhythm with words such as "very good", "very fine" etc. Again she sings as she goes and is quite relaxed.

158

25th October: We discover that a few days ago Renée started eating with a spoon. Till then she was fed with a thin puree. Now she eats more solid food with her own hands, but still very slowly. That she eats and feeds herself can be appraised as an affirmation of life, she *wants* to eat, a sign of the will to live.

In the session she held the beaters in her hand for 25 minutes (we heard that she also held the spoon for some time in her hand). Cautiously she takes the hoop, she turns the upright hoop round once, she does it with her left hand and with her right hand and while she does it she sings something like:

As she went out she sang a complete melody. This showed that she was now able to walk more easily:

26th October: If one lays out all the different coloured beaters for her she always takes a pair of the same colour, red, blue or grey.

On the soprano xylophone she plays a particular note in a particular rhythm and then changes to another note, always repeating the rhythm on one note only.

She plays a different rhythm on the bongos:

Playing with a partner in a gesture imitation game with beaters she spontaneously crossed her beaters, changing them backwards

159

and forwards, sometimes with the left in front and sometimes the right. During the whole session she threw nothing away. Her stereotype chin-beating, beater twiddling and absent staring have as good as disappeared. In her own room if she is not being addressed in some way she reverts immediately to these movements.

30th October: She is now always pleased when one fetches her. She relates actively to a partner. She imitates gestures reliably. If she makes some opening gesture and this may sometimes be only an awaiting attitude – perhaps to interlock her hands behind her head – the therapist copies this movement to make her aware of it.

Nine months have passed and twenty-five music therapy sessions have taken place. A child who was unable to make contact, and who expressed herself only in stereotype behaviour, has grown into a girl who can relate to companions, who has movement ideas and movement reactions that can be described as meaningful to offer. She has learnt to stand, to walk, she expresses herself increasingly in vocal sounds and not stereotype ones, she has eye contact, she watches, she imitates, she distinguishes between contrasts, she knows when she wants something, and she makes demands. Her development is slow but steady. It is interesting to be with her. She has her own level and everyone who sees her is impressed. In spite of limited forms of expression she is, within the scope of her possibilities, intelligent. She remembers – and this is the first intellectual accomplishment.* With a careful selection of new challenges on the part of the therapist, and through working at the girl's reactions, one will be able to expect more from her. The vocal expression will increase and before that she should be able to walk freely. She rewards every consideration of the path that her therapy should take with new accomplishments.

★ Lutz, J.: *Probleme des behinderten Kindes,* Urban u. Schwarzenberg, München 1973.

10. The secret of the therapy

By secret we mean something that does not lie exposed in the foreground, and that is therefore not accessible as a matter of course. Secret has something to do with depth, kernel and dark, terms that also have to do with growth. What does therapy have to do with secret?

The therapy process is carried out before our eyes with tangible material, in play with forms, with gesture, with speech, sound and notes. Therapy is activity and the effect of the activity. The activity lies open, the effect is carried out in concealment. When and in what way the impulses that we give in music therapy arrive, eludes the enquiring therapist. The reaction of a child is a sign that the impulse has found its mark, the absence of a reaction does not mean that the impulse has had no effect. A surface reaction does not have to reach the depths, an impulse that reaches the depths can do so without any external reaction.

In therapy with an autistic child things can happen inside him that are not visible. Also in therapy with a child with a severe mental handicap something can stir that is not to be seen outwardly. The time factor of the reaction is different. Thus reactions of autistic children are often quicker and differently stored from what the therapist imagines, the place of penetration remains a secret: where the therapist expects a child to look round, she gets only the blink of an eyelid. With the mentally handicapped child reactions are delayed, longer than the norm, so that the therapist often does not wait for the reaction. Reactions from blind and deaf children are different again.

The therapy is carried out in a condition of meeting, the situation is that of being face to face or opposite, but also of being in opposition: child–adult, needy–helper, taker–giver. In the last pair of opposites if a sign of the reversibility shows itself, an ebbing of the effective process, they become like one another, they change with one another. He who first did the taking now makes an offer, the first impulse now comes from the child, the therapist reacts. The situation of opposite one another changes to next to one another and with one another. It changes from a subjective to an objective relationship. The objective experience can only take place after the subjective.

161

In group therapy the initial central place taken by the therapist is changed to a shifting central place, each one has a turn at being in the centre, with the attention focused entirely on him when he leads an imitation or when he handles the theme of some game. The role of central place is passed around and often comes to one un-expectedly. The secret of the group therapy lies in the flexibility of this central place. Through this an evening out of levels can be achieved, the over-loud are put back, the shy dare to come forward. The free handling of the central place, the open situation, the shifting of the balance, the balancing of the different weights, produce, together with other things the specific atmosphere. The experience of community through common activity, the free setting of im-pulses that arise from the children, the demanding of decisions – and this is also possible with three-year-olds – produces this par-ticular atmosphere, whose secret it is that it is effective, that it enlivens, that it intensifies, that it mitigates and calms. The atmo-sphere acquires its particular colouring, its stimulus, and its whole-someness through the movement, the perpetual, unobtrusive rhythmic flow and the sound colours that are produced in various ways. One can analyse this situation but one cannot always bring it about. It is always the gift of that particular session.

The secret of bringing it about lies in trusting the good moment, the good session. It is achieved through good preparation, thorough meditation about the individual members of the group and in the tolerant, active holding together of the session that places the therapist on an invisible watchtower. The decision lies with her and her flexibility.

The secret also lies in the possibility of active involvement from the very beginning in our Orff Music Therapy, to act, to play, to decide, spontaneously to grasp the creative moment – what will come out of this, what will the result be? In a condition of tension one is on the scent of the secret. Exploration is motivation to activity, the aesthetic develops itself from the energetic impulse. This is the first thing. Giving life to the atmosphere in the group or in the individual session brings about a spontaneous activity, that is right because it comes from the animation. But one cannot reckon with the animation, it has to arise of itself. When and if it arises remains secret. This helps the therapist not to fall back on her successes, recipes and techniques. She remains alert. That which is apparent in the therapy can be foreseen, reckoned with and expected. Therapy, however, cannot exist only out of what is apparent.

It was established at the beginning that what is essential to the Orff Music Therapy is that in the first session the dice are cast, that in the first session a positive relationship should be developing, and a positive affect should appear. It is this *affect* that produces the end condition of *effect*. *Facies*, the Latin word for face, expression, comes from the word *facio*, I do. Doing and the effect of doing leave their impression on the face.

What happens in reality is fulfilled in the word. The priority of word and reality is not touched upon here. For those for whom a word is a signpost, the word has priority: the contact with a word has released an affect, that has its effect in the carrying out of the way. The traversing of the way with its experience can be contained within the word, the word then houses the way. Word and way are a secret.